P9-CKV-853

EDWARD F. DOLAN, JR.

DRUGS IN SPORTS

A GROLIER COMPANY

FRANKLIN WATTS
NEW YORK LONDON TORONTO SYDNEY 1986

WITHDRAWN

Photographs courtesy of:
AP/Wide World: pp. 8, 9,
25, 39, 55, 64, 85;
Allsport/Tony Duffy: p. 18;
Drug Enforcement Administration:
pp. 46, 72, 95;
Raoul Vega/Major League
Baseball Association: p. 103.

Library of Congress Cataloging in Publication Data

Dolan, Edward F., 1924–
Drugs in sports.

Bibliography: p.
Includes index.
Summary: Describes the widespread use of anabolic
steroids, brake drugs, amphetamines, cocaine, and
marijuana by athletes and discusses what the sports
world has done to cope with drug abuse.
1. Doping in sports—Juvenile literature.
2. Athletes—Drug use—Juvenile literature.
[1. Athletes—Drug use. 2. Drug abuse] I. Title.
RC1230.D65 1986   362.2'93'088796   85-29521
ISBN 0-531-10157-6

Copyright © 1986 by Edward F. Dolan, Jr.
All rights reserved
Printed in the United States of America
7 8 9 10 11

CONTENTS

Introduction
Drugs in Sports
1

Chapter One
Going for the Winning Edge
4

Chapter Two
Anabolic Steroids: A Health Menace
14

Chapter Three
Anabolic Steroids: Broken Bodies, Troubled Minds
23

Chapter Four
Anabolic Steroids: Why Athletes Risk Them
34

Chapter Five
The Amphetamines
44

Chapter Six
The Amphetamines in Sports
53

Chapter Seven
Braking and Boosting
62

Chapter Eight
Cocaine: The Drug of the 1980s
71

Chapter Nine
Cocaine and the Athlete
80

Chapter Ten
Marijuana
91

Chapter Eleven
Working to Stop the Problem
100

Further Reading
117

Index
120

DRUGS

IN SPORTS

INTRODUCTION
DRUGS
IN SPORTS

As anyone who reads a newspaper or watches a television news program cannot help but know, today's world is suffering a major drug problem. Though drugs have been used since perhaps the dawn of time, today's problem was born in the late 1950s and early 1960s. It was triggered by a number of complex social factors, chief among them the stresses of the times. In the years since its birth, the problem has spread to all parts of the globe and to all walks of life, touching people of all ages as it has gone along.

Among the millions who have felt its touch are the vigorous people who are to be the subjects of this book—the world's athletes. Many have been caught up in the abuse of the so-called recreational drugs—cocaine, marijuana, and alcohol, to mention just three. Many have used legitimate medical drugs as training aids, but in ways and to extents that add up to a dangerous misuse, a misuse that can do—and has already done—extensive physical and psychological harm. The abuse and misuse have ruined careers and have severely damaged the reputation of sports throughout the world.

It must be said at the outset that not all athletes are involved in the problem. There are competitors everywhere who want to have nothing to do with drugs. But the problem is there, and has become so widespread over the years that it is now found among athletes at every level of competition—from world-class amateurs and highly paid professionals to high school and even junior high school performers.

It is an ugly and tragic problem that must be faced and discussed if it is somehow to be solved. And face it is what we plan to do in this book. We're going to look at all aspects of the problem—at the major drugs being misused and abused, at the harm they can do, at the athletes who risk that harm, and at the reasons why so many athletes feel driven to run that awful risk. Then we'll talk about what a troubled sports world is doing in an effort to end the misuse and abuse.

The problem is not only ugly and tragic but also complex, and so I have needed much assistance in the preparation of this book. A word of appreciation is owed to everyone who has helped.

In particular, I wish to thank Drs. Anthony Maddalo, M.D., and Gilbert W. Gleim, Ph.D., of the Institute of Sports Medicine and Athletic Trauma at Lenox Hill Hospital in New York City for reviewing the manuscript of this book to check that all the medical information in it is accurately stated.

And, for providing me with needed sports and drug research materials and for answering specific questions, I wish to thank the offices of: the National Football League, the National League of Professional Baseball Clubs, the Major League Baseball Players Association, the Major League Player Relations Committee, the National Hockey League, and the Drug Enforcement Administration of the United States government. I also must thank the *Washington Post* newspaper for kindly permitting me to quote from articles on drug abuse in sports that appeared in its pages in 1979.

The purpose of this book is to acquaint you with the dangerous drugs that are found in sports today, so that, armed with an understanding of their hazards, you may be able to make some contribution to ending their misuse and abuse. Perhaps you'll do so by talking with an athlete friend who is toying with them; perhaps by spreading the news among all your friends so that they, too, may take some kind of action; or perhaps—most important of all—by keeping these drugs out of your own life if you are an athlete.

Whatever action you take will be of great help. Misuse and abuse have become a health menace throughout the sports world. They are a menace that must be recognized and somehow eradicated if sports are to continue being what they have always been intended to be—healthful, enjoyable, and fair contests of physical prowess and skill.

Edward F. Dolan, Jr.

CHAPTER ONE

GOING FOR
THE
WINNING EDGE

Popeye is weak and tired. He needs something to give him quick energy, bulging muscles, and superhuman strength. . . . He pulls out a can of spinach and gulps down its contents. Presto. No one, not even the bully Bluto, can stop him now.

With these words, journalist Barry Lorge began a series of articles for the *Washington Post* newspaper in the nation's capital. The articles appeared in 1979. They dealt with today's widespread and troubling problem of drugs in sports.

The reporter wrote on: "It is not that simple outside of cartoons, of course. But nevertheless, athletes for generations have been searching for that elusive can of spinach."

In that brief paragraph, Lorge pointed out a basic fact: though his articles were to be about a modern problem, there is nothing new about drugs in athletics. As is true of the world at large, drugs have been a part of the sports world for centuries. Their history there has been the same as in the larger world. They've been employed for legitimate medical purposes. They've often been misused—that is, taken too often or in quantities too great for safety. And they've often been abused in the search for pleasure or an escape from life's trials.

And, as is so true in the world at large, the presence of drugs in the sports world today is greater than ever before. The reasons for this are the same in both worlds. Modern science has developed more drugs—and for a wider variety of medical problems—than were ever dreamed of in earlier ages. Modern means of transportation and distribution have made these myriad drugs more readily available to greater numbers of people than ever before. The pressures and strains of daily life seem especially sharp at present. The result: In increasing number and with increasing frequency, the two worlds have turned to the vast and readily available drug supply—sometimes for legitimate medical use, sometimes for misuse, and sometimes for outright abuse.

No one can deny that drugs, when wisely employed for medical purposes, are among the greatest boons ever given humankind. They have done everything from relieve everyday aches and pains to eradicate some of the world's most feared diseases. It is the misuse and the outright abuse of drugs that have caused the trouble throughout the long centuries. They lie at the root of today's drug problem in both the world at large and the sports world.

Not all athletes, of course, misuse or abuse drugs, or even take them at all. Nevertheless, so great has the sports misuse and abuse become during recent years that it is now being called an international disaster. It has done physical and psychological damage to athletes of both sexes, of all nationalities, and at all levels of competition—from the highly paid professional to the beginning amateur. It has even brought death at times. It has damaged the very nature of sports, twisting many of the world's best-loved games and events into anything but the healthful, exciting, and fair contests of skill and prowess that they were intended to be.

In this book, we are going to look at all aspects of this disaster. To begin, let's turn again to what Barry Lorge called "that elusive can of spinach." It was his way of pointing to the drugs at the core of the problem.

DRUGS AND SPORTS

The world's drugs can be divided into two basic types—the medical drugs and the drugs of abuse.

As we all know, the medical drugs available today are so legion as to seem countless. They vary in strength from mild, everyday medications that can be purchased over the counter in drugstores to highly potent and dangerous substances that require a doctor's prescription and careful medical administration.

In sports, the medical drugs are more likely to be misused than abused. Misuse can occur in any of several ways. For example, it often comes after an athlete obtains a legal prescription from a doctor to take a drug as an aid to his or her training. The athlete then wants more and more of the drug, all with the idea that a greater benefit will accrue. But the doctor, knowing the hazards of increased use, refuses to cooperate. Frustrated, the athlete turns to other sources—friends, fellow competitors, even the illegal drug market—for the needed supply. Free of medical supervision, the drug is almost always taken with greater frequency and in larger and larger doses.

Another example: The athlete doesn't obtain a doctor's prescription in the first place. Perhaps he or she feels that the physician will object to the drug as too dangerous for use. Or perhaps the athlete sees no need to seek out a doctor. The drug is being handed out by a friend, a fellow athlete, or a dealer.

No matter how the misuse occurs, it threatens damage to the body and mind because prolonged, heavy, and unsupervised doses bring all the dangerous effects of any potent drug to the forefront. That damage can be terrible. Sometimes, the misuse is so great that it adds up to abuse.

And what of drugs of abuse? In sports as elsewhere, they are usually taken for pleasure or to escape the trials that life brings. The drugs of abuse are usually referred to as the "recreational drugs," a term that strikes many people as a sad commentary on modern life. How, they ask, can the obvious harms done by these drugs correspond at all with the idea of recreation and the healthful pleasures it is supposed to bring? Nevertheless, the term is widely used and accepted. Ranking highest among the popular recreational drugs of the 1980s are cocaine and marijuana.

Within the sports world itself, various medical drugs have long been used. Like the drugs of the larger world, they, too, can be divided into two basic types.

First, there are the drugs intended for the athlete who is unable to perform up to his or her usual standard. Perhaps he or she is under some sort of heavy strain that interferes with effective performance. Or perhaps there has been an injury of some kind. Whatever the case, these drugs are meant to help the athlete return to normal or perform in spite of the problem.

Heading this type are such drugs as pain-killers, tranquilizers, sedatives, and balms to reduce and soothe inflammations and muscle stiffness. Many are everyday drugs that do no harm when sensibly used.

The second type consists of drugs that *add* to the athlete's prowess. Their aim is to help the athlete perform beyond the level that he or she might reach without their aid. The athlete turns to these drugs in the hope that they will provide that all-important element in competition—the winning edge. Desired by all competitors—and desired *above all else* by some—it's the vital extra "something" that helps them to best the competition, outdo themselves, and become champions.

Over: Runner Mary Decker in the 3,000-meter race and Edwin Moses after winning the finals of the men's 400-meter hurdles. Both athletes took part in the 1984 Olympic Games in Los Angeles. Many outstanding athletes have made it to the top of their sport without the use of drugs.

7

Just how do these drugs provide that edge? Some do the job by adding physical strength. Some by instilling energy. And some by lifting the spirits and fostering strong feelings of self-confidence.

Because of such capabilities, the winning-edge drugs are extremely powerful and, consequently, dangerous substances. And also because of these capabilities, they are the medical drugs most misused in athletics today. In sum, they are the present-day counterpart of Barry Lorge's "elusive can of spinach."

GOING FOR THE EDGE

The desire for that winning edge which will help make you a champion is one of the main forces behind today's drug problem in sports. This desire has for centuries been a force behind the use of drugs in sports. It is a principal reason (if not *the* principal reason) why athletes have always tried to open that elusive can of spinach. Reporter Lorge quite correctly calls it "elusive," because the perfect drug, the one that will give the edge without hurting the user, has yet to be found.

Their quest for that drug has caused the athletes to write an always strange and sometimes dangerous history. Over the years, they've tried everything from the most useless to the most lethal of concoctions.

For example, insofar as useless mixtures are concerned, many athletes of ancient times felt certain that strength and stamina came from drinking a liquid made of the crushed hooves of an Abyssinian ass. The hooves were boiled in oil along with some rose petals.

Not so useless, however, were the ashes from the burned leaves of South America's coca tree. The Inca Indians found that the ashes, when held in the mouth, somehow fired the body with great energy and made sleep unnecessary for several hours or even several days. The Incas used them when faced with tiring battles, hunts, and sporting competitions. Today, we know that the ashes contained the stimulant drug, cocaine.

For generations, the Kaffir tribesmen of South Africa

used a ceremonial drink called *dop* when engaged in war or athletics. Brewed of alcohol and cola, dop was supposed to provide extra energy and stamina. When the Boers settled in South Africa, they made the term a part of their language. However, they added an *e* to it and gave us the word that has come to mean all drugs: *dope.*

The mid-nineteenth century saw the beginnings of today's widespread development and manufacture of drugs. As the new drugs emerged from the laboratories of the day, many were tested by eager athletes in various nations. The French tried caffeine. The Belgians thought that ether would improve their performance; they managed to swallow the foul-tasting stuff by placing dabs of it on sugar cubes. A number of runners, on hearing that nitroglycerine causes the coronary arteries to dilate, felt that it could help them improve their speed. They reasoned that the widened arteries would allow more blood to reach the heart. In turn, the heart would beat faster. The result: a faster pace. Nothing of the sort happened. For their trouble, the runners won nothing but violent headaches.

Racing cyclists in several European countries dreamed up an extra-energy recipe they called the "speedball." Stirred into it were two of nature's most deadly drugs—cocaine and heroin. In 1886, the pair demonstrated just how deadly they were by taking the life of a cyclist in a cross-country endurance event. His was the first drug-related death ever recorded in sports.

Tom Hicks of the United States was luckier. Minutes after winning the marathon event in the 1904 Olympics, he collapsed. When the runner finally regained consciousness with the help of four doctors, it was found that he had fed himself something quite as dangerous as a speedball. Hicks had downed a mixture of strychnine (a deadly poison in overdose) and brandy.

Damage and death, as we'll see in later chapters, have continued to this day as athletes have persisted in experimenting with drugs that promise the winning edge by increasing strength, stamina, and confidence.

TODAY'S WINNING-EDGE DRUGS

Today, in the winning-edge drug category, you'll find three especially potent and dangerous entries—the anabolic steroids, the amphetamines, and what are called "brake drugs."

The anabolic steroids are hormonal drugs that are thought to provide increased strength by building new body tissue. The amphetamines are chemical mixtures used for extra energy and confidence. The brake drugs suppress—put the "brakes" on—certain physical developments. Said by sports experts to be used principally in Eastern Europe, they serve to keep women gymnasts small and lithe.

A medical procedure, though it involves no drugs whatsoever, must also be placed in the same category as the drugs just mentioned. It is called "blood boosting." Some doctors think it creates increased energy by pumping additional red cells into the athlete's system. It also helps by increasing the blood's oxygen-carrying capacity.

Even the so-called recreational drugs have come to be viewed as winning-edge drugs by many athletes. Cocaine is seen as advantageous by some because of the sudden thrust of energy and confidence that it provides. Some athletes turn to the depressant effects of marijuana to help them come down from the energy highs of cocaine and the amphetamines or to quiet the tensions of waiting for tomorrow's game.

THE COMING PAGES

In the coming pages, there will not be sufficient space to concentrate on every drug that has found a place in sports. There will be no need to mention the mildest of the lotions and balms that ease the pains of injury and stress. Nor will we talk about the various drugs that are used by just a few athletes. Among such drugs are the relaxants manufactured under such brand names as Valium and Raudixin. They are often a help to archers, golfers, and firearms marksmen who wish to steady their. hands.

Rather, our attention will go to the drugs that are misused or abused by the greatest number of athletes—drugs that also happen to do the greatest harm because of their potency. In turn, we'll look at the medical drugs eagerly sought in the hope of gaining that all-important winning edge: (1) the anabolic steroids, (2) the amphetamines, and (3) the brake drugs. Then we'll turn to the nondrug procedure, blood boosting, and go from there to the abuse of today's chief recreational drugs—cocaine and marijuana. For reasons that will be explained cocaine is due to receive a greater share of attention than marijuana.

Throughout the book, we'll have five questions uppermost in mind:

1. What do these drugs contain?

2. How do they work on the body and mind?

3. What physical and psychological harms can they do?

4. Why do many athletes turn to these drugs when their dangers are so well known?

5. What is the sports world doing to curb or halt today's widespread misuse and abuse of drugs?

Let's consider these questions first as they relate to the collection of drugs whose misuse is said to have reached epidemic proportions worldwide—the anabolic steroids.

CHAPTER TWO

ANABOLIC STEROIDS: A HEALTH MENACE

The dark-haired body builder was twenty-three years old. With rippling muscles and broad shoulders, he looked to be in glowing health. But, suddenly, he began to show the signs of liver disease. His skin turned yellow. A severe itch plagued his entire body. One night he became so ill that his parents rushed him to the hospital. The doctors there found the young athlete to be suffering from liver-kidney failure. He died four days later.*

At age twenty-two, the woman was blond and slim. Her sport was basketball. She was practicing and exercising daily in the hope of making the women's team in the 1984 Olympics. Over a period of several months, she was appalled to see her muscles beginning to bulge too much. She heard her voice grow deeper as time went by. A darkish stain broke out on her upper lip. It was the beginnings of a moustache. Horrified, the young woman felt that she was turning into a man.

Larry Pacifico is a world-class powerlifter. He holds a record nine consecutive world titles in his sport. All were won between 1971 and 1979. In 1981, at age thirty-five, Pacifico underwent surgery on his elbow. Afterward, while yet in the hospital recovery room, he was struck with a

---

*Death in the Locker Room, by Bob Goldman, with Patricia Bush and Ronald Klatz. South Bend, IN: Icarus Press, 1984.

heart attack. An examination showed that two of the arteries to his heart had become 70 percent blocked. A third artery was 99.9 percent blocked. Pacifico was luckier than the young body builder. He did not die. An operation helped to save his life.

ONE THING IN COMMON

These three competitors came from different sports. Each trained in his or her own way. But they all had one thing in common. They had taken some form of the drugs known as anabolic steroids.

The three were not drug abusers. They had not been looking for the "kicks," "highs," and escapes from reality to be found in the recreational drugs. Rather, they had turned to the anabolic steroids for help. They knew them to be substances with an amazing ability—the ability to build new body tissue quickly. New body tissue would bring increased strength. In the increased strength, the trio hoped to find that winning edge—that invaluable extra something that would help them best all the competition.

But the drugs seem to have backfired. Since the steroids were the one thing that the three athletes shared, it struck everyone that they must have been behind all the trouble. The hospital doctors blamed them for the liver-kidney failure that had killed the young body builder. The woman basketball star was sure that they were making her look more and more like a man. Larry Pacifico was equally certain that they had caused the blockage of his arteries.

The three cases are frightening. But they are far from unusual. The anabolic steroids were first developed in Europe in the 1930s. They were intended and initially used for medical purposes only. Then a few athletes in search of that all-important winning edge began to experiment with them. Since then, steroid use in sports has fanned out to all parts of the world. It is a use that has revealed the steroids to be not only amazing body builders but also drugs with the ability to do terrible physical and psychological damage. A steadily increasing number of sports and medical authorities are coming to see their spread as a worldwide health menace.

EARLY STEROID USE

When they were first developed, the anabolic steroids were thought by doctors to be "miracle drugs." Their ability to build new tissue made them superb medications for patients recovering from starvation and for the victims of severe injury. They also did much to prevent the withering of muscle tissue in patients forced to remain inactive for long periods after surgery. In addition, research found that they could be helpful to girls suffering the delayed arrival of puberty. Today, the steroids continue to serve these same medical purposes.

Because of their marvelous body-building capabilities, the steroids could not long escape the eye of the sports world. Athletic experimentation with them was under way by the mid-1950s and may have begun several years earlier. Exact dates cannot be given here because the first sports use took place in countries behind the Communist Iron Curtain. It was kept a secret from the Western world. Soon, however, the whispered word was leaking out that here were drugs that could increase strength and give their users a real edge.

The word seemed true. Russian weight lifters were among the first to use the steroids. Aided by the drugs and state-sponsored training programs that provided ample hours for workouts, the lifters developed into massive and powerful athletes. The result: They dominated their sport worldwide for years.

Soon, however, the steroids began to be unmasked as anything but helpful to athletes. Ever since the drugs had first appeared, research into their effects on the body had been conducted on animals and humans. As yet, the research was far from complete (it is still far from complete as you read this book), but the indications were that the steroids were dangerous. Especially if not taken under strict medical supervision, they could harm a user in various ugly ways. And, as appeared to be the case in the tragedy of the young bodybuilder, they seemed able to kill.

THE SPREAD OF A PROBLEM

Yet, despite all the frightening indications, a steadily growing number of athletes turned to the anabolic steroids over the years, sometimes with medical supervision and sometimes with no supervision whatsoever as they tried them on their own after being supplied by fellow competitors and others. From the first experimentation behind the Iron Curtain, steroid use spread to the rest of Europe and then to areas beyond the sea, among them the United States and Canada. The earliest use appears to have been limited mainly to weight lifters and powerlifters. Since then, though it must always be stressed that not all athletes are users, the steroids have found their way into a wide variety of sports, including track, football, and basketball.

For a number of years, use was pretty much limited to the elite of the sports world—to competitors striving for national and international titles. Many sports meets have long employed saliva and urine tests to see that the competitors neither jeopardize their health nor gain an unfair advantage by taking certain drugs. Failure to pass the tests results in disqualification from the meet. These tests have revealed some of the world's finest athletes to be steroid users.

In the late 1970s, for example, two great women track-and-field stars—East Germany's Ilone Slupianek and Russia's Nadezhda Tkachenko—were made to surrender the medals they had won in international competition. Slupianek lost the gold medal she had taken in the shot put at the 1977 European Cup meet, while Tkachenko had to surrender the gold for the pentathlon in the 1978 European Championships. At about the same time, Russian swimmer Viktor Kuznetsov lost his bronze medal won for the 100-meter backstroke at the West Berlin swimming championships. Discus thrower Markku Tuokko

of Finland had to give up his gold medal in the 1977 European Cup.

More recently, the International Weight Lifting Federation disqualified nine steroid users during a mid-1980s world championship meet held in Ohio. Even worse, fifteen world-class competitors in lifting and track-and-field were expelled from the 1983 Pan American Games at Caracas, Venezuela, when steroids were detected in their systems. Surrendered by the fifteen were twenty-three medals.

The Ohio and Venezuela disqualifications did more than show that steroids were being used by many top-flight athletes. They also left no doubt as to how far steroid use had spread in the world. Disqualified at Ohio and Caracas were competitors representing fourteen nations—Argentina, Canada, Chile, Colombia, Cuba, the Dominican Republic, Hungary, Japan, Nicaragua, Poland, Puerto Rico, the Soviet Union, the United States, and Venezuela.

Today, steroid use is no longer limited to the elite of the sports world. The passing years have seen it spread to athletes of all ages at all levels of competition—to any competitor who wants, above all else, that winning edge. Studies and news reports show that today's users range from world-class amateurs and highly paid professionals to college, high school, and even junior high school performers.

While it must always be stressed that not all athletes take the drugs—or any drugs whatsoever—steroid use has now, in the words of Dr. Clayton Thomas of the Olympic Sports Medicine Council, reached epidemic proportions internationally.

Steroid use in Eastern European sports produced a number of extremely powerful female athletes such as the shot-putter shown here.

EPIDEMIC PROPORTIONS

No one can say exactly how many athletes have turned to steroids in recent years. But a statement by Dr. James Wright, a well-known authority in sports medicine, can give us an idea of just how widespread the use must be. A 1982 issue of *Sports Illustrated* magazine reported Dr. Wright as saying that 70 to 80 percent of the steroids in the United States are not being used for their original purpose of healing illness and injury. Rather, they are being taken by the already-strong to increase prowess.

The statements of some top-notch competitors can tell us even more about the extent of use. A track-and-field star in the 1980 Olympics says that many athletes would have dropped out of the Games had the word gone round that some new test had been developed and could expose anyone who had ever used the drugs. (The Olympic Games, looking on steroid use as dangerous and unfair, have been disqualifying users since 1973.) A professional football player believes that anyone who graduated from college and entered the professional ranks in the past four years has tried steroids. A college powerlifter flatly admits that every lifter of his acquaintance is a user. A California letterman in several high school sports says that one of his coaches put him on steroids.

(In the early days of steroid use, some coaches and trainers gave their athletes steroids without a doctor's advice and supervision because they did not understand what the drugs could do. They stopped the practice when the steroid hazards became better known. Today, the coaches and trainers who continue to obtain and give the steroids on their own are thought to be relatively few in number and are roundly criticized by their more sensible colleagues. A principal charge leveled against them is that they are so eager for victory or a championship that they'll risk the health of their athletes to achieve it.)

The epidemic of steroid use is being seen by many medical and sports authorities as one of the greatest menaces in the current drug problem because the research into the steroids continues to make their awful dangers clearer and clearer. We'll be looking at those dangers in a few pages. In the meantime, we need to know some basic facts about the steroids themselves.

WHAT ARE
ANABOLIC STEROIDS?

The answer to this question begins when we define each of the two words in the term *anabolic steroid*. *Anabolic* means the ability to promote body growth and repair body tissue. It comes from the Greek word *anabolikos,* meaning "constructive." *Steroid* refers to a number of compounds of a certain chemical nature.

The basic chemicals that make up the steroid compounds are the body substances called *hormones.* These hormones may be given to an individual in their natural state. They may be given as *synthetics,* meaning that their natural structure has been altered in the laboratory to make them better able to perform certain medical tasks. There are also steroids in which hormones are not actually present. Such steroids are composed of chemicals that, when mixed together, achieve the same results as the hormones.

Different kinds of hormones can be used in steroids. One kind, for example, comes from the adrenal glands, which are located just above the kidneys and secrete various needed body chemicals. Another kind is progesterone, a hormone found in females. Still another is testosterone, which is found principally in males. Some steroids are made of combinations of different hormones.

In sum, then, anabolic steroids are drugs that come from hormones (or from combinations of chemicals that achieve the same results as the hormones) and that prompt the growth of healthy body tissue. They are manufactured today in a number of forms—as powders and tablets to be taken orally, and as liquids to be injected into the muscles.

Many types of steroids have been produced through the years to treat various illnesses and disorders. One of the best known of all is cortisone, a medication used in the treatment of problems ranging from rheumatoid arthritis and rheumatic fever to a number of allergic conditions. The medication, cortisone, is one of the many hormones made by the adrenal glands.

A SPECIAL POINT

One last point must be stressed. In the main, of all the different steroids available today, the ones taken by athletes contain testosterone or chemicals that act as it does. As mentioned above, testosterone is found in men. It is produced in the testicles. It is also found in women, but in much smaller amounts. In the coming pages, we'll be talking almost always about the steroids that spring from this particular hormone. Today, more than 120 testosterone steroids are marketed throughout the world. They are manufactured under a variety of brand names. Among the better-known names are Durabolin, Winstrol, Pregnyl, and Anavar.

And now it's time to talk in detail of the steroid dangers. They are dangers that loom for both the body and the mind.

CHAPTER THREE

ANABOLIC STEROIDS: BROKEN BODIES, TROUBLED MINDS

The anabolic steroids can be called "dual personality" drugs. On the one hand, they are able to do fine medical work. But, on the other, especially if carelessly used, they can harm. Their harms are known as "side effects," because they are results other than the ones that use is intended to bring. The steroids resemble many another valuable medical drug in their dual personality. One example is the splendid pain-killer, morphine. It must always be handled with extreme caution because it has addictive side effects that can enslave a patient.

Despite their dangers, the steroids can be obtained over the counter in some countries—that is, they can be bought at drugstores or markets by anyone, just as if they were aspirin or a cough remedy. In other nations, where the drug control laws are stricter, the potent side effects are recognized and the steroids can be had only with a doctor's prescription. The United States is one of the countries requiring a doctor's prescription.

DOCTORS AND STEROIDS

Along with doctors elsewhere in the world, physicians in the United States who deal with athletes differ in their views of steroid consumption. Some will not prescribe the drugs at all for sports use, regarding them as too dangerous to be given to perfectly healthy individuals.

Some refuse prescriptions on the grounds that the swallowing of some pills to gain a winning edge adds up to cheating. And some see them as unnecessary for top athletic performance. Along with all the athletes, coaches, and trainers who oppose any sort of drug use, they feel that good diet, healthful living habits, and steady train- · ing are the elements best able to ensure a sparkling performance.

But other physicians are willing to prescribe the steroids for adult athletes and do so for a variety of reasons. Some consider the drugs safe when administered under medical supervision—a supervision that carefully regulates the dosages and then quickly adjusts them or ends the use at the first sign of trouble.

Others don't like the steroids, but understand that many an eager competitor will seek them from other sources if refused a prescription. Those sources are all too many and all too easy to reach on today's world-wide drug scene—friends, fellow athletes, trainers and coaches, the black market, and drugstores in those countries where the steroids can be legally purchased over the counter. Understanding all this, the doctors reluctantly go ahead and authorize the drug's use rather than let the athlete risk taking it on his or her own. At the least, they are then able to supervise its administration and watch for trouble.

Still other doctors recognize the possible serious harms, but say that everyone does not necessarily suffer those harms. They point out that even aspirin, one of the least dangerous of all drugs, can do damage. But millions of people take aspirin safely because its possible harms are generally slight and experienced by relatively few users, while its pain-killing capabilities are great. The physicians here feel much the same way about steroid use under medical supervision. They feel that the use may well not harm most athletes because they are in such fine physical shape and that it can be stopped if harm does begin to show itself. They feel that the body-building benefits to be won outweigh the risks involved.

Who has the right idea here? The doctor who re-

Weight lifters were among the first athletes to experiment with steroids, but drug use was still no guarantee of victory.

fuses to prescribe the steroids? Or the doctor who writes a prescription? There is no final answer—and may never be. It is all a matter of medical opinion and judgment on the part of the individual physicians.

But one point is certain. Research and the experience of users leave no doubt that the greatest harm has been done when athletes have obtained the steroids on their own and used them without medical supervision.

What has happened to these athletes? Almost invariably, not knowing what amounts can be taken with reasonable safety, the athletes have downed far too much of the drug, perhaps right from the start. And in keeping with the general points made about misuse in Chapter One, they have almost invariably increased the dosages as they've gone along. They've told themselves that the continuing use and the increased dosages would reap greater benefits.

As potent as the steroids are, prolonged use of small amounts can be dangerous. Extended use of heavy amounts may prove to be lethal. What we'll see in the next pages is the havoc that prolonged use—especially prolonged heavy use—has wrought.

Basically, but in very complicated ways, the anabolic steroids raise this havoc by upsetting the body's chemistry and hormonal balance. The upset results from jamming the system with excess testosterone (or, in those compounds that do not actually contain testosterone, with chemicals that act like it). The upset causes the same kinds of damage in both males and females. But there are special harms done to women alone. And special harms just for men. Let's look at these various damages in turn.

MEN AND WOMEN IN DANGER

To begin, some doctors suspect that anabolic steroids bring on—or help to bring on—heart attacks by causing the arteries to harden and thicken. The result is *arteriosclerosis,* the condition that almost killed Larry Pacifico. It has also been found that the steroids prompt the body to retain too much water. This retention leads to a rising blood pressure that, if left unattended, can lead to a heart attack or stroke. A stroke occurs when a blood vessel bursts in the brain.

The noted researcher in anabolic steroids, Bob Goldman, explains how the steroids drive the body to retain water in dangerous amounts. In his book, *Death in the Locker Room,* Goldman points to the basic fact that our bodies contain a number of chemicals, among them chlorine, sodium, potassium, and nitrogen. A certain amount of water is needed to balance these chemicals. The steroids cause us to retain too much nitrogen. To balance things out, the body begins to retain more water. A strain is put on the blood vessels because they must now pump increased amounts of fluid through the system. Up goes the blood pressure. In time, the strain proves beyond endurance. The heart gives out or a blood vessel snaps in the brain.

And there is an allied problem. The increased amount of fluid causes the body to expand with what athletes have come to call "steroid bloat." They try to right things by taking diuretics, medications that empty the fluid through excessive urination. The diuretics may help to end the bloat, but in at least one instance, their use has ended in tragedy.

Recently, a young California weight lifter died of a heart attack after using steroids for some months. When doctors conducted a postmortem on his body, they found that he had also been taking diuretics in large dosages. They induced a urination so heavy that it purged his system of electrolytes. These are chemicals (a chief one is potassium) that assist in regulating the heartbeat. Once they were too far reduced, his heart had been unable to endure the resultant irregularity.

Current research, along with user experiences, strongly indicates that steroids can either cause or help to cause cancerous tumors in the liver and possibly in the kidneys. And as in the case of the twenty-two-year-old body builder, they are suspected of bringing on liver and kidney failure.

Though supposed to develop and strengthen muscle tissue, the steroids seem just as capable of destroying it. The destruction seems especially prevalent among weight lifters. Eric Hoffman, long a major figure in United States lifting, wrote of the problem in an article published by *Sports Illustrated* magazine in 1982.

Hoffman said that muscle and tendon injuries were rare in his sport until lifters began taking steroids. Now, such injuries are commonplace, with the biceps (in the arm) and the quadriceps (at the front of the thigh) being the muscles most frequently harmed. Hoffman reported that scores of lifters have suffered the experience of seeing their biceps muscle roll up the arm "like a windowshade" after the tendon holding it to the bone broke away. Others have collapsed during training or competition when the tendons holding their quadriceps in place gave way.

In young athletes who have not yet reached their full height, the steroids are accused of causing acne (doing the same thing in some adults) and halting bone growth.

All the damage that is done is usually not reversible—meaning that it will not disappear when usage is stopped—when the steroids have been taken heavily for prolonged periods. Some types of damage are reversible in light or infrequent steroid users.

WOMEN IN DANGER

To see the special hazards for women, we have to add a new term to the definition of anabolic steroids containing testosterone or chemicals that act like testosterone. They are not only body-building and tissue-repairing drugs, but also *androgenic* drugs. An androgenic substance—also called an *androgen*—is one that promotes the signs of masculinity. It brings on the development of the male sex organs and is responsible for the man's beard, body hair, and deep voice. It is likewise behind the male's heavy muscle mass. In the main, the steroids prompt this building of weight and muscle mass by increasing the body's ability to absorb protein.

Obviously, these steroids promote the signs of masculinity, because, though some testosterone is naturally produced in females, it is a male hormone.

In women, the small amount of testosterone is kept in balance with the *estrogens,* the hormones that give a woman her feminine characteristics and regulate her reproductive cycle. Additional amounts of testosterone rapidly destroy this balance, with the result that she begins to show, as did the young Olympic basketball hopeful, a series of male characteristics.

The woman sees the gentle curves of her body begin to vanish, to be replaced by hard and bulging masses of muscle. Weight is gained. The voice deepens. The skin roughens. A moustache appears. Baldness may occur.

(Men likewise experience the roughening of the skin and the growth of excess hair. The hair, looking as if it better belongs to King Kong, appears in dark splashes on various parts of the body.)

The changes seen in a woman may not be reversible once well started. Further, their onset cannot be prevented should the woman try to hold them off or counterbalance them by using drugs containing the female hormone, estrogen. In fact, studies indicate that women face an increased danger of certain cancers when using steroids while taking birth control pills. These contraceptives all contain estrogen.

The woman is not alone in running the risk of all the changes. Her unborn children are also in danger. In *Death in the Locker Room,* Bob Goldman writes that the female baby still in the uterus of a woman taking steroids will develop such male traits as extra hair. Also, many doctors suspect that steroid use may lead the women to giving birth to deformed and handicapped children.

This suspicion has yet to be confirmed through research. But it is strong enough to have caused a number of women competitors to fear having children. As one California athlete has said, "I really want to have children. But I'm afraid to. I just don't know how normal they would be. The whole thing scares me to death."

In addition to all these dangers, women run the increased risk of breast cancer.

MEN IN DANGER

Many male athletes have experienced a shrinking (called *atrophy*) of the testicles. In a number of cases, this condition has been accompanied by a falling sperm count, a lessening of sexual desire, and infertility (the inability to father a child).

Some male athletes have suffered an enlargement of the prostate gland (the gland that produces the fluid in which the male sperm resides). The condition is a painful one that is not usually found in men under age fifty.

Quite often the male user develops breasts like those of a woman.

THE MIND IN DANGER

Research into the manner in which the steroids affect the user's personality is showing that they act in much the same way as the amphetamine drugs. Amphetamines are chemical mixtures that erase fatigue, fill the user with energy, and enable him or her to perform tirelessly for long hours. When the drugs wear off, the user enters a period of exhaustion that is often accompanied by feelings of deep depression. Extended use of the amphetamines, as we'll see in a later chapter, can enduce chronic depression, irrational behavior, and hallucinations.

Athletes who have taken steroids say that, along with providing gains in strength, the drugs made them feel energetic, tough, and confident. They became more aggressive in both training and competition, wanting even more than before to be champion performers. So far as many athletes are concerned, these feelings are all to the good. As they see it, the feelings have added to that winning edge.

But if this is indeed the case, the steroids have at the same time exacted a terrible psychological price.

Users have felt—and their friends have seen—wild swings in mood. In moments, the athletes have gone flashing from heights of confidence and happiness to lows of depression and anger. Many have found themselves sleeping restlessly. Some of the most easygoing of individuals have watched their natural sense of competitiveness turn into a sharp, and even dangerous, hostility toward their opponents in meets and games.

A recent issue of *Sports Illustrated* reported on the change in one quiet-spoken athlete, a professional football player. Though always tough on the field, he said that he had never wished serious harm on an opponent. But now, on being hit hard, especially with what he called "cheap shots," he really went after the opponent with every intention of hurting him in ways he had never dared before.

This new hostility was not limited to opponents. The player's wife noted that he just as quickly became hostile off the field, that he talked louder and more angrily than before, and that he had become very rough in their lovemaking.

Energy and confidence are necessary for successful participation in sports. But the steroids provide so much that, aside from doing psychological damage, they have led to physical injuries. Muscles and tendons have been damaged when the users have driven themselves to train too long and too hard. (Some of the earlier-mentioned bicep and quadricep injuries suffered by weight lifters may have been caused by unwise overtraining.) Most athletes have a "sixth sense" that tells them when they've worked enough for the day. The steroids, handing out an excess of energy and confidence, have deadened that sixth sense.

It is unknown as yet whether the steroids, like such drugs as morphine and heroin, are physically addictive. But there is evidence to suggest that they may be psychologically addictive—that an athlete may so come to depend on their uplift and body-building capabilities that he or she feels unable to compete without their help.

An example of this kind of dependence is provided

by one user athlete who later became a sports official. He admits to knowing that the steroids almost killed him, but says that he couldn't give them up when he returned to competition. He felt that he could no longer win without them—even though he had been a champion performer long before ever hearing of steroids.

Other athletes have faced such problems when trying to drop the steroid habit that they've wept. The close friends of one athlete are certain that he became suicidal because of the effects of the steroids and the difficulties involved with quitting.

One reason why it is difficult to drop the steroid habit has to do with a certain way that the drugs act. The steroids are effective only when they are in the system. As soon as they are stopped, much of the gain in strength and tissue growth is lost. The loss comes, no matter how hard the athlete trains to prevent it. Having won the great gains, many users can't stand the thought of losing them.

IGNORING THE DANGERS

The physical and psychological dangers of steroid use are showing themselves to be so awful that medical and sports authorities everywhere are loudly condemning them.

Bob Goldman, for example, told *Time* magazine that any competitor who experiments with steroids is "playing with dynamite." He added that steroid users are not just risking health problems but also death. The American College of Sports Medicine has called for a broad program to educate athletes, coaches, trainers, physicians, and the general public on the hazards of steroid use.

Yet, in spite of these statements—and many others like them—the use of steroids to build new body tissue and enhance strength and performance has continued to grow through the years until, to repeat the words of Dr. Clayton Thomas of the U.S. Olympic Sports Medicine Council, it has reached epidemic proportions. Joining Dr. Thomas in this view is Dr. Daniel Hanley of the

U.S. Olympic Committee. He says that the problem of steroid use is worse today than ever before.

When faced with so much ugly evidence, why have more and more athletes turned to the steroids? Are they blind? Stupid? Or has their need to win overcome all else and driven them to take any risk for the sake of a future victory?

The possible answers to these questions are given in our next chapter.

CHAPTER FOUR

ANABOLIC STEROIDS: WHY ATHLETES RISK THEM

During the early years of their history, the steroids were most often taken in ignorance. At the time, little was understood of their possible dangers. Many users simply did not realize that they were venturing into hazardous territory.

But matters are different today. The word of what the steroids can do is now widely known in the sports world. It has been spread by news reports in such magazines as *Time* and *Sports Illustrated.* It has been spread by such books as *Death in the Locker Room* by Bob Goldman, *The Sportsmedicine Book* by Dr. Gabe Mirkin, and *Anabolic Steroids and Sports,* Volume I and II, by Dr. James Wright. And perhaps most effectively of all, it has been spread by athletes who are personally acquainted with the steroids—by competitors who themselves have had unhappy encounters with them or have seen their user friends suffer.

As a result, many users have abandoned the drugs. But just as many others—perhaps even more—have ignored the warnings. And still other athletes, though fully aware of Bob Goldman's caution that they are "playing with dynamite," have begun the steroid habit.

What drives today's users to risk their health and even their lives by challenging the steroid dangers? The answer has two parts. First, it involves certain personality traits found in many athletes, especially in those who desire, above all else, to be champions. Second, it has to do with a number of pressures exerted by the sports world on modern competitors.

We'll look at each part in turn.

THE "MUST WIN" PERSONALITY

Let's say that you participate in a sport because it gives you pleasure. You like to win, yes. Who doesn't? But winning isn't everything. What really counts is that you get to join in the fun and enjoy the companionship of your fellow players. For you, a sport is just one part of life— a fun part, indeed, but still just one part.

Millions of people the world over participate in sports in this way. But they differ greatly from the truly dedicated athlete, the athlete who wants to go as far as possible in his or her sport, who yearns to take bigger and bigger championships, and who dreams of perhaps turning professional one day. Most—if, indeed, not all— truly dedicated athletes are said by psychologists to have compulsive personalities. Success in their sport means *everything* to them. They feel compelled to win. Many see themselves as failures as human beings if they lose.

It is this compulsiveness that drives the truly dedicated to train long hours, endure tiredness and hunger, and give up much time that could be spent relaxing with friends. They make these sacrifices because they love what they are doing, want to win, and want to be the best there is.

On the one hand, the deep-seated need to win and do your best is great. It accounts for many of the splendid achievements made in all lines of endeavor. But, on the other hand, it is a desire that can be dangerous if it is not handled sensibly—and this is what has happened to so many athletes who have tried steroids, especially those who have taken them without medical supervision.

It has driven some to risk any danger just to get that winning edge. One ambitious weight lifter recalls a terrible experience. "I saw one of my friends collapse on the platform during a meet. His left quadricep had given out. We were both on steroids and I knew the same thing could happen to me. But I never considered stopping them. I just had to take my chances."

The same compulsion has driven some athletes to the steroids because their competitors were on them. Speaking to this point, another weight lifter remembers, "When I heard that a major opponent in my weight class had started steroids, I could think of just one thing. He's getting a big advantage. He's going to win. I couldn't let him get away with it."

And it has driven some individuals to increase their steroid consumption and thus worsen their problems. Today, a former college football star shakes his head at what he calls his "total dumbness" as he says, "I saw the great body gains that came with just a few tablets. And so I told myself, hey man, if a couple of tablets will do this much good, then twice as many will do twice as much good."

Just how deep this compulsiveness can run in the athletic personality is seen in a story told by Dr. Gabe Mirkin, the author of *The Sportsmedicine Book*. Dr. Mirkin, himself an excellent runner, recalls the time he asked one hundred runners if they would take a drug that would make them Olympic champions but would kill them in a year.

More than half the runners shocked him with their answer. It was yes.

In *Death in the Locker Room,* Bob Goldman writes that he was as shocked as Dr. Mirkin by that answer. He wondered if it really represented the feeling of a wide body of athletes. He decided to formulate a question of his own for 198 of his friends, most of whom were weight lifters. He asked them if they would take a drug that would enable them to win every championship meet for the next five years, even if they knew it would kill them at the end of that time.

Goldman reported that 103—or 52 percent—of the athletes expressed a willingness to take the drug. He said they understood that its use would amount to cheating because of the unfair advantage it gave. Still, they were willing to take the drug and willing to give their lives for the thrill of winning.

THE ATHLETIC MIND-SET

In addition to a compulsive personality, many hard-driving competitors develop what is called the "athletic mind-set."

The term springs from the fact that athletes train hard for a single goal or a series of goals. Perhaps the single goal is an Olympic gold medal. Perhaps the series of goals adds up to a string of victories that carry the individual from local to national and then international competitions—or to the ranks of the professionals. Soon, it's all too easy for the athletes to think of nothing else. Put yourself in their place and you'll likely hear yourself saying, "I must get where I'm going—at *any cost.*"

The case of a young woman body builder in the Midwest serves as a fine illustration of what can happen here. She believed in the traditional approach to winning championships—the developing of skills, stamina, and strength through rigorous training, proper diet, and sufficient sleep.

But her friends told her that she was falling behind because her competitors were all on steroids. What chance, they asked, did she have of reaching her goal— a national championship—when her competition was getting the edge with chemical help. *She had to catch up.* At first, she shook her head adamantly. But soon the pressure and the desire to achieve her goal proved too much. She tried her first steroids.

She regrets her decision to this day, saying that the harm far outweighed the benefits.

A PRESSURE WORLD

The woman body builder had to endure the pressures exerted by her friends. All dedicated athletes—especially those questing after significant championships or a place in the professional ranks—have to endure some heavy pressures exerted by the sports world itself.

People have always loved sports. It's a love that can be traced back to ancient times—back to the Egyptians who enjoyed a form of bowling some seven thousand years ago, back to the Greeks who crowded in to see the first Olympic Games about thirty-four hundred years ago, and back to the Chinese who played a soccerlike game twenty-five hundred or so years ago. But, though it has always been there and though it has always been great, the love of sports is especially keen and wide-spread in our day. People everywhere are fascinated by athletics.

Our modern means of communication are greatly—if not mainly—responsible for this fascination. Daily, the press, television, and radio inform us of what's going on throughout the athletic world and, in so doing, have often made us fans of sports that we previously knew nothing about. They report immediately on the outcome of games and meets held anywhere on earth. Better yet, radio and television allow us to follow the meets and games as they take place. Just how many spectators can "attend" a sporting event and share in its thrills without leaving home was clearly seen in the 1984 Summer Olympics at Los Angeles, California. Loving every minute of the action, more than 2,500 million people across the world watched the Games unfold on television.

But the Olympics are not the only athletic attractions that draw huge audiences. In the United States alone, several million people annually attend or tune in to college basketball and football games. And millions more are avid followers of professional sports—football, baseball, basketball, hockey, tennis, and golf, to name just a few. Even high school events that once pulled in perhaps several hundred spectators are now watched by several thousand in those cities where the competitions are telecast by local stations.

All this attention has made superheroes of athletes—especially the very top competitors. Their names are known to millions. As professionals, they command

*The winning edge is often mental
in nature. An ability to focus on
the goal at hand can separate a winning
performance from a second-best effort.
Weight lifters exemplify the importance
of mental concentration.*

salaries that can stagger the imagination. Every fan has read of outstanding amateurs who sign professional contracts worth millions of dollars. It's common knowledge that even the average salaries in the pro football, baseball, and basketball leagues are on a par with—and often exceed—those paid to top business executives. And every TV viewer knows that top performers from both the amateur and professional ranks have the chance to appear in commercials, work as sports commentators, write books as Jim Bouton and John Brodie have done, and even, as in the cases of Alex Karras and Jim Brown, become acting stars. One of today's most firmly established facts is that success in sports can lead to a lifetime of fame and highly paid work.

And so the athletes feel a great pressure. They must always perform at their best if they hope to reach championship or professional status and the rewards to be found there. Then, on arrival, they must go on performing at their best and winning if they hope to continue reaping those rewards. As a result, many ambitious young competitors have turned to the steroids for help on the climb up the ladder. And many amateur and professional stars already at the top, growing older and nearing the end of their careers, have used the steroids in the hope of finding the strength that will enable them to remain in the limelight for as long as possible.

As if all this were not enough, there is a further pressure. It is exerted on athletes in international meets—competitors who are representing not just their teams or their schools, but are out there on the court or the field for their countries.

THE INTERNATIONAL PROBLEM

International meets were originally intended to promote understanding and friendship among the peoples of the world by bringing their best athletes together in amicable competitions. Through no fault of the athletes or of people in general, that intention has long been threatened. Global politics have been at fault. For years, they have intruded on the meets and have sought to make them political rather than sports events. In 1936, for example, when the Olympic Games were held in Germany, dictator Adolf Hitler planned to have his athletes post a series of triumphs that would prove the Germans to be, as he so loudly insisted, the world's "master race." Hitler's fury was reported everywhere when his plan was upset by America's splendid black track star, Jesse Owens. The dictator damaged the spirit and intent of the Games by turning his back when Owens stood proudly on the winner's stand to accept his three gold medals.

But, as bad as it was, the damage done to the 1936 Games in no way could match the damage that world politics have done to international events in the years since World War II—the years of the Cold War between the countries of the free and Communist worlds. Increasingly, political forces have turned competitions such as the Olympics into power struggles between nations—especially between the United States and the Soviet Union—rather than tests of athletic skill and prowess. The result has been to twist the purpose of the meets until, in the minds of far too many people, they now mean: "My country won more medals than your country, and so my country is better and stronger than yours." In effect, this situation has turned the athletes into warriors. They *must* win to prove not only their personal ability but their nation's worth.

It's a situation that makes no sense. What does an individual's ability to run, jump, or pole-vault have to do with the basic worth of his or her country? How can failure to win a medal lower that basic worth? But the situation nevertheless exists.

It irks countless fans and troubles all those athletes who share a deep camaraderie with their foreign competitors and want nothing more than pure contests of skill and prowess. And it has brought us to the point where some people felt that there would be no excitement in the 1980 Olympics when the United States, angry over the Soviet invasion of Afghanistan, refused to send a team to Moscow. There was the same feeling four years later when the Russians retaliated (with the excuse that their athletes would not be adequately protected while in Los Angeles) by boycotting the 1984 Games.

Senseless though it is, the situation has put an extra pressure to win on the international competitors and has been one more factor in prompting many of them to the use of steroids. The fact is that international political rivalries have long played a part in the steroid problem. They have been on the scene right from the beginning. As you'll recall from Chapter One, the drugs were initially used in the countries behind the Iron Curtain. It was the sense of international "sports warfare" that caused these countries to keep secret the word of the steroids. They wanted that winning edge all to themselves.

The rivalries were again seen as the word of the steroids fanned out across the world. As the secret of these "wonder drugs" leaked out, the coaches, trainers, and athletes of other nations were quick to try them in the hopes of snatching the winning edge away from the Communist-bloc countries. Such was the case with the first steroid use in the United States.

Steroids were introduced into the United States by the late Dr. John Ziegler, a fine physician, scientist, and athlete. Long a leading figure in United States weight lifting, Dr. Ziegler traveled to Vienna, Austria, for a 1956 championship meet. One evening while there, he went to dinner with a Russian trainer who was also a close friend. The trainer told him that the Soviet athletes had found some miracle drugs—called anabolic steroids—and were realizing tremendous strength gains from them.

Dr. Ziegler was angry that the Soviets had grabbed such an advantage. He also felt that the Russians were planning to use sports to help prove their political superiority to the world. Wanting to help his country keep up with the Soviets, the physician came home with the news of the steroids, prescribed their use for his weight lifter friends, and worked with the CIBA Pharmaceutical Company of New Jersey to develop the first American steroid, which was marketed under the brand name, Dianabol.

The doctor was always careful in his administration of the steroids. But, in time, he saw the compulsive athletic nature at work. Some of the competitors in his care asked for larger and larger doses. When he refused, several obtained the drug from other sources, joining a growing number of athletes who were using it on their own. And, in time, he saw the harm that the steroids could do and turned against them. The CIBA Company, also seeing the harm, discontinued the production of Dianabol, although the firm today manufactures other steroids.

Dr. Ziegler died in 1984. Just before his death, the man who had brought the word of the steroids home so that his nation could stay abreast of the Soviet competition said that he wished he had never heard of the things.

We've now come to the spot where we can talk about the third point in the steroid problem—what the sports world is doing to halt its spread. We're going to save our discussion of this point until later in the book, however. At that time, we'll be able to talk not only about it but also about the steps being taken to combat the use of other drugs in sports.

And what are those other drugs? We'll begin to look at them now.

CHAPTER FIVE

THE
AMPHETAMINES

This chapter begins with the work of a Chinese emperor who lived four thousand years ago. His name was Shen Nung. A scientist as well as a ruler, he studied and wrote about a number of plants. They possessed, in the emperor's words, "magical powers" that could relieve the suffering of the sick and injured. One was a bush that he called *ma huang.*

Shen Nung described *ma huang* as a low, woody shrub with clusters of green twigs. On the twigs bloomed the tiny leaves and flowers that gave the plant its "magic." If a man, Shen Nung wrote, stirred them into a tea, he would concoct a potion that could lower a fever, improve his circulation, and give him a feeling of well-being.

Today, we know *ma huang* to be the Ephedra plant, which grows mainly in desert regions and is nicknamed the horsetail plant. And we know that its active agent—the substance responsible for those "magical powers"—is the alkaloid ephedrine. Ephedrine is defined as a vasopressor, meaning that it stimulates the heart and circulation. Out of it have come a number of drugs that, because of these stimulating effects, are widely used in the treatment of low blood pressure, shock, and Addisonian anemia. A variety of mild ephedrine drugs, when inhaled, have proved of value in the relief of hay fever, asthma, and nasal congestion.

Scientists invented a synthetic form of ephedrine in

the late nineteenth century. It emerged as a drug that, like Shen Nung's *ma huang,* provides a strong sense of well-being and fires the body with energy. They christened it amphetamine. The term comes from the structural name of the chemical *alpha-methyl-phenethyl* plus *amine* (*amine* means a type of organic compound).

In the years since its invention, amphetamine has been developed into some thirty different drugs, with their differences depending on the chemical mixtures involved. They have been manufactured as tablets, capsules, inhalants, and liquids. The various amphetamines are marketed today under such brand names as Dexedrine, Mediatric, and Desoxyn.

THE ENERGY GIVERS

The amphetamines are classed as stimulant drugs because they instill that same sense of well-being—of uplift—that Shen Nung noted in *ma huang.* But it would be an understatement to say that they just make a person feel good. They do far more. They lower one's sensitivity to pain, erase the need for sleep, and fill the user with a bounding energy. This energy has earned them such familiar nicknames as uppers, wire, and pep pills. They also have nicknames that rise from the shapes of the various pills, their colors, their contents, and the rates of their action—footballs, greenies, black beauties, dexies and bennies (for the brand names, Dexedrine and Benzedrine), and speed (for the quick-acting methamphetamine). Users have traditionally been known as "speed freaks."

Though their history dates back to the late nineteenth century, the amphetamines were not introduced into medical practice until the 1930s. Since then, they have helped the ill in a number of ways. They have long served, for instance, in the treatment of *narcolepsy,* a rare disease that triggers the overwhelming need to sleep. They have also been used to enliven patients whose physical or emotional illnesses are causing a serious loss of energy. And, because they curb one's hun-

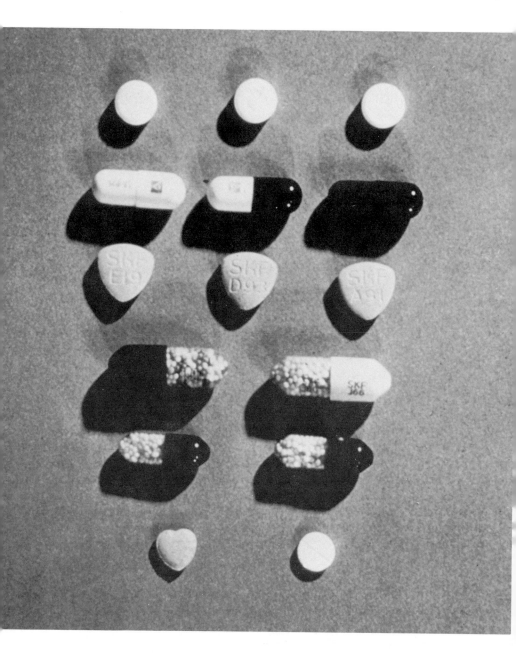

Amphetamines

ger while imparting their feelings of energy, the amphetamines are prescribed for weight loss in certain cases of obesity.

For some odd reason that medical science has yet to understand, one amphetamine drug, methylphenidate, acts in reverse when given to hyperactive children. Rather than energizing the youngsters, it calms them. And so the drug plays a role in the treatment of children's *hyperkinesis,* a brain disorder marked by constant activity and the inability to concentrate.

Their energizing abilities have seen the amphetamines widely employed in preventative medicine over the years. In the main, they have been prescribed to help safeguard individuals who must remain awake and perform well if they are to have a good chance of getting through times of exhausting physical and mental strain. Ever since World War II, many nations have distributed amphetamines to military personnel in battle. The astronauts aboard the ill-fated Apollo 13 moonshot in 1970 took amphetamines to keep them alert throughout the long return to earth after an oxygen tank ruptured in their spacecraft.

For some years after being introduced into medicine, the amphetamines could be had without a doctor's prescription. Easily obtained over the counter at drugstores, they were eagerly sought out by anyone needing extra energy. Truck drivers bought them to stay awake on long hauls. So did students who had to study through the night for a morning exam. And so did actors, musicians, and factory workers faced with a tiring night's work. But in the years following World War II, the potency of the amphetamines began to be recognized and the government declared that they could be secured only with a doctor's prescription. However, their use was not placed under the strictest of controls and they remained readily available. By 1970, the government had come to regard the amphetamines as truly dangerous drugs. As part of an overall revision of United States drug laws, Congress adopted strict regulations surrounding their administration.

THE AMPHETAMINES AT WORK

The amphetamines work by releasing two chemicals—epinephrine and norepinephrine—from the adrenal glands and the nervous system. On release, these chemicals cause the muscles to tense, the heart to beat faster, and the blood pressure to rise. The result: The user feels energized, wide awake, and capable of much activity. Depending on the dosage taken, the period of energy and wakefulness can run from several hours to two or three days. It is, of course, followed by an extreme tiredness and the need to sleep.

When taken in small amounts or just occasionally, the amphetamines are not considered especially dangerous. Their dangers come with heavy and continued use—the sort of use most frequently seen when they are not administered under careful medical supervision.

Heavy and continued use is especially dangerous because the body quickly builds a tolerance to the drugs. It requires them in increasing doses to reach the same energy highs previously achieved with lesser amounts. The amphetamines, however, are not categorized as physically addictive substances. This is because when use is stopped, it does not bring on the painful withdrawal symptoms associated with other drugs—for example, the sweating, the runny eyes and noses, and the contorted intestines that occur with heroin withdrawal. But there is no doubt that the amphetamines are psychologically addictive, with the user often coming to think that he or she cannot function successfully without their help.

ENERGY OUT OF CONTROL

What happens with heavy and continued use? In a nutshell, the amphetamine energy gets out of control. Users start to behave in various odd ways. Imagine for a moment that you are an amphetamine user, and consider what you will experience. You'll likely find that you simply cannot remain still, but must be up and pacing here and there. You'll also probably be hit with the over-

whelming urge to talk—and talk and talk. In time, you may become the victim of a condition that drives you to repeat pointless tasks or actions over and over again. You may, for instance, find yourself walking in endless circles just to be doing something. Or you may string beads for hours without knowing what you're doing, turn the pages of a book without seeing them, or write the same word a thousand or more times.

And, in time, you're more than likely to find that all the unleashed energy did not allow you to do what you set out to do. You may have wanted the energy for writing a term paper that you let go until the night before it was due. Throughout the night, you write away and think that you're doing a brilliant job. Then, on coming down from your high, you're shocked to see what you've written. It's all gibberish.

Or, if you're a truck driver, you may think that you're in top form, in full control, as you roar through the darkness—only to wake up hours later in a hospital and find that you were tragically mistaken. Studies show that drivers who are heavy users suffer more accidents than nonusers, often because of their erratic behavior, often because they suddenly fall asleep when the effects of the drug wear off.

Or, if you're a football player, you may behave as a defensive lineman did one afternoon. He infuriated his coaches when, on every play, he charged to the exact same spot in the enemy backfield. The opposing team quickly took advantage of his strange habit and aimed all plays away from that spot. Time and again, the man was ordered to change his tactics. But he was powerless to obey and went on blindly repeating himself. At last, he had to be pulled out of the game.

Or, if you're a baseball player, you might suffer the experience of the big league pitcher whom Jim Bouton mentions in his book, *Ball Four*. The man felt that he was having a great day on the mound. He was sure that he had never pitched better. In fact, he was sure that he was throwing the ball as well as any big-leaguer had ever thrown it. Then the manager walked out to the mound

and told him that his last three pitches had been tagged for home runs. Shaking his head in disbelief, the pitcher headed for the showers.

As a heavy and habitual user, you may well begin to hallucinate, seeing or hearing things that aren't there. The hallucinations are usually anything but pleasant. The personnel in drug treatment centers regularly see amphetamine victims who scream that strange bugs are crawling all over them. On recovering, one such victim was astonished to learn that the "bugs" had been bits of dried skin on his arms.

No matter whether you're a heavy or a light user, you fall into a deep sleep when the drug wears off and you come down from the energy high. The letdown grows increasingly difficult for the habitual user. After the sleep, there may be the awareness of the foolish things you did, and certainly the awareness that the drug did no real good and that you're trapped in its use. These understandings can bring a deep depression and a sense of self-loathing that, in time, can become chronic. Many users, knowing the agonies that letdown can bring, take other drugs to make things easier for themselves by dulling their senses. Among the drugs most used at these times are alcohol, the barbiturates, and the treacherously addictive narcotic, heroin. The barbiturates and heroin are depressant drugs, meaning that they suppress body actions and bring on sleep.

By turning to such drugs, you begin to create an "up-and-down" pattern of usage that is all too familiar in the amphetamine world. Chronically depressed, you use the amphetamines to find some energy, then the depressants to help you back down, and then the amphetamines again for the next trip up.

The mental illness called *paranoia* often results from heavy and continued use. Here, your wakefulness and alertness take an odd turn. They make you suspicious of everyone around you. You begin to think that all the people you see—friends and strangers alike—are out to harm you in some way. Perhaps they want to cheat you, perhaps make fun of you, perhaps hurt you physically,

perhaps even kill you. In your twisted state, you're likely to attack the suspected persons or lock yourself up at home and hide from them.

On top of all else, heavy and continued use poses the threat of death. An overdose can be—and often has been—fatal. There have been several instances of soccer and football players collapsing and dying on the field after downing too much of the drug. Further, because the amphetamines curb the appetite, some users have wasted away to the point where they no longer had the resistance to stave off or survive an illness. And any medical worker who has dealt with amphetamine use can tell you of the suicides that have resulted from the deep depression brought on by the drug.

AMPHETAMINE ABUSE

In the years before and immediately following World War II, there was little amphetamine abuse, either by athletes or the general public. The amphetamines were used, yes, but chiefly for medical purposes. Public abuse—that is, remember, the heavy use for pleasure or an escape from life's burdens—began in the late 1950s and early 1960s, those turbulent years that saw the birth of today's worldwide drug problem. By the close of the 1960s, the abuse of the amphetamines ranked right alongside that of the far more publicized drugs of the day—marijuana and LSD.

At that time, no one knew (and still no one knows) exactly how many people were abusing amphetamines. Law enforcement authorities and drug experts, however, believed that the total ran into the millions. Studies and police records showed that the users came from all walks of life and ranged from the very young (there were cases on record of preteen users) to the very old.

Some idea of how great the illegal use must have been can be had by looking at one fact. In the late 1960s, some ten billion amphetamine pills were being manufactured annually in the United States for legitimate medical purposes. At least half those pills "disap-

peared" each year and found their way into the illegal drug trade. They arrived there after being stolen from manufacturers' warehouses, from hospitals, from doctors' offices, drugstores, and even home medicine cabinets.

The amphetamines continue to this day to be widely abused by the public, although they've taken a backseat to another stimulant—the most popular illegal drug of the 1980s, cocaine. Still, worldwide, the illegal amphetamine trade, fed by stolen pills and by those produced in clandestine factories (located mainly in Europe and Latin America), reaps a multimillion dollar harvest each year. In the United States alone, the illegal sale of the amphetamines and such other drugs as the methaquaaludes (widely abused tranquilizing drugs) is estimated to be worth about $17 billion annually.

The 1950s and 1960s saw the amphetamines become as popular with athletes as with the public. This was to be expected. Competitors who had never heard of the things before now listened eagerly to the news of all the great energy to be had. Here was another way to gain that winning edge. They went for it. Since then, many of their number have suffered the harm that increasing misuse has wrought, a fact that brings us to our next chapter.

CHAPTER SIX

THE AMPHETAMINES IN SPORTS

Though they have likely been abused by some athletes for pleasure or to escape life's problems, the amphetamines have been mostly sought after in sports as winning-edge drugs. As such, they have long been used legally. Legal use, as you know, requires a doctor's prescription.

As winning-edge drugs, the amphetamines have mainly been prescribed in those sports that call for a tremendous amount of stamina and endurance. Cyclists facing long races, for instance, have taken them. So have football, soccer, and baseball players readying themselves for an afternoon of hard action. The same goes for track-and-field competitors in need of a sudden burst of energy.

Similarly, the amphetamines have been used in sports that make weight demands on the competitors. To mention just three examples, they have been prescribed for boxers, wrestlers, and jockeys dieting to make weight requirements.

And, as winning-edge drugs, the amphetamines have been called on to serve the needs of certain athletes at certain times. Here we're talking about players who, as Barry Lorge wrote in his series of *Washington Post* articles, are "going all out in the last period of any exhausting game" and competitors who are up against almost unendurable demands:

a cross-country skier or cyclist facing the last hills of a grueling journey . . . a 35-year-old football player who no longer has the spring in his legs of the 25-year-old across the line from him . . . a sprinter who has to toe the mark in a meet where fractions of a second loom unimaginably long . . . a sore-armed relief pitcher trying to get through the last days of a 162 game season . . . or a javelin thrower who knows that an Olympic medal depends on one's backlog of quality training, and needs a little extra pep to get him through the days when he doesn't feel like training.

Of the sports mentioned above, football must be singled out for extra attention. Here amphetamine use seems to be especially widespread, particularly in the professional ranks. In fact, amphetamine use in professional football is widely recognized by sports authorities as being a greater and more enduring problem than in pro baseball, basketball, and hockey. There are two reasons for this. First, the game is a hard-hitting, bone-crunching test of strength (in many ways, even a harsher test than hockey). The players know that the pain-killing capabilities of the amphetamines will help them to take and dish out the game's continual and jarring hits.

That the amphetamines are used to dull pain can be seen from the player positions where they are said to be most used. Studies show that linemen are more likely than backfield men to be amphetamine users. Special teams, famous for the bruising punishment that they must absorb, also have a reputation as users. For years, they have been known within the National Football League as "greeny squads."

Second, there is the nature of the game itself. Players know that it is most successfully played when there is confidence and a sense of controlled anger. The amphetamines help to provide that confidence and controlled anger.

The amphetamines are said to be especially popu-

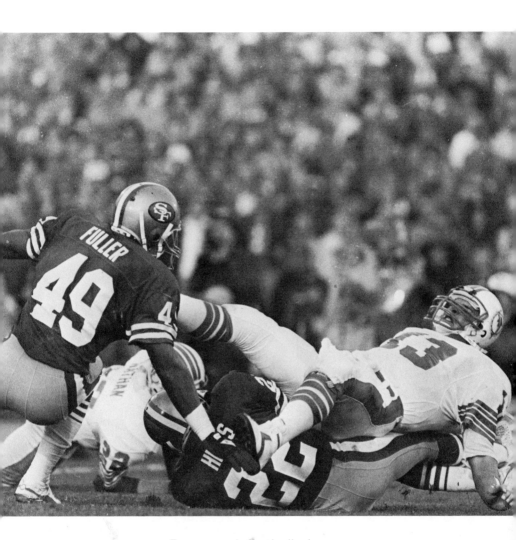

Every week football players suffer body-crushing blows as they seek to outplay their opponents. Amphetamines have been used by some players in the sport to dull the pain of injuries and "fire up" a flagging mental attitude.

lar among older professional football players. In the eyes of most doctors, the reason for this popularity is obvious. As one doctor has put it, "The older player's body has taken years of punishment and is feeling the cumulative effects. And age is catching up with him. He's not as able to absorb punishment as he was ten years ago. And he knows it. The amphetamines dull the pain and give him the feeling that, for at least a little while longer, he's as good as he ever was."

Another reason is theorized by Dr. Arnold Mandell, a research psychiatrist and a former consultant to the San Diego Chargers. Mandell believes that the controlled rage is connected to certain brain chemicals whose actions decrease with advancing age. He says that it is quite easy for, say, a nineteen-year-old to "psyche" himself up—gather that controlled rage—for a game. But the rage builds more slowly and reaches lower heights as the years go by. As Dr. Mandell sees it, the player in his mid-thirties is simply unable to make himself angry enough. He then turns to the amphetamines to bring on the anger that the brain chemicals once induced so easily.

A CHANGE FROM EARLIER DAYS

But now one important point must be made. Though they can be legally prescribed, the amphetamines are not as much used today as they once were. In the 1960s, before their dangers were fully recognized and before the government's 1970 adoption of strict regulations concerning their use, uppers were freely dispensed in American locker rooms, especially those at the professional level. Just listen to some of the memories from that time:

Baseball's Johnny Bench was just breaking into the major leagues. He recalls that the team trainers always had Dexamyl and Darprisal pills (two popular brand names) in ample supply. In his autobiography, *Catch You Later,* he writes that no one, neither trainer nor player, was concerned about handing them out in generous quantities before gametime.

Similar recollections come from professional football and basketball. Several National Football League veterans, among them tight end Jean Fugett, say that when they entered play in the late 1960s or early 1970s, amphetamine use was commonplace. It was not considered especially dangerous and was joked about by their fellow players. In a 1979 interview for the *Washington Post,* pro basketball star Paul Silas said that the taking of uppers was widespread among players when he joined the National Basketball Association in 1964.

Silas, however, pointed out that amphetamine use in the NBA has dropped significantly since then. He said that years ago many players lived too hard off the court, staying up late to drink and play cards. Exhausted the next day, they turned to the stimulants to get "up" for a game. But now they are making astronomical salaries, and they're meeting their responsibilities to those salaries by taking care of themselves. As Silas sees it, they no longer need the help of the pills. Additionally, he mentioned the speed and mental sharpness required for pro basketball. Silas said flatly that players simply can't handle the game's lightning-fast action and constant demand for quick thinking if they're downing what he called "all kinds of stuff."

The move away from the heavy use of the 1960s began early in the 1970s. In 1970 itself, the United States replaced its earlier drug laws with the Comprehensive Drug Abuse Prevention and Control Act. The act set forth strict regulations for the production, sale, and use of all dangerous drugs—narcotics, stimulants, depressants, and hallucinogens (drugs able to make a user hallucinate). As stimulants, the amphetamines were included in the act. As had been the case during the years following World War II, they were to be available only with a doctor's prescription, but were now to be more strictly regulated than ever before in their administration. The major professional sports groups—the two baseball leagues, the National Football League, the National Basketball Association, and the National Hockey League—quickly responded to the act. Concerned over the growing drug problem in sports, they all established antidrug policies (we'll see exactly what they did when we come to Chapter Eleven). The amphetamines were affected in two ways by the policies. The leagues began routinely checking the amounts prescribed by team physicians, a practice that has continued ever since. And team physicians and trainers were charged with taking extra care in their administering of the drugs.

THE PROBLEM REMAINS

But despite all these steps, the amphetamine problem did not disappear. The situation remained the same, as with other winning-edge drugs. Those players who wanted more amphetamines than could be legitimately obtained turned to outside sources, including the illegal market, for their supplies. And the result? It is the same as with other drugs: an undisciplined and unsupervised misuse.

This misuse netted some sad consequences. Since an increase in a player's aggressiveness can go hand in hand with his rising energy, the suspicion is widespread that heavy amphetamine use is behind some exceptionally rough football action that has ended in injury. Further, a number of football and baseball players suspect that they've seen paranoid behavior during games. In the faces of some teammates and opponents, they've glimpsed expressions that go beyond the intensity that is normal in the heat of competition. As one player has put it, "Those guys looked and acted as if they hated you. You felt they were trying to get back at you for some dirt you had done them. I like hard play, but not that kind. It's downright dangerous."

These are all suspicions. They're bad enough. But there are proven cases of the harm that the amphetamines have done.

Reporter Barry Lorge, in his 1979 series on drugs for the *Washington Post,* dwelt on one especially sad case. It concerned a California track-and-field star who, as Lorge reported, "became accustomed to popping a couple of uppers before every track meet in Long Beach, where he was the leading high school shot-putter in the country in 1973. He increased his drug intake during an ill-fated college career, and went on several legendary drug-induced rampages.

"The most notorious came after the 1976 Pacific-Eight Conference championships." The athlete, a star at the University of California at Los Angeles (UCLA) was favored to win the shot put, but "came in a disappointing second. Although fortified by a massive dose of amphetamine, he 'unwound' with tranquilizers and then, in the words of a witness, 'just went berserk.' "

Lorge wrote that the athlete, who weighed more than three hundred pounds (140 kg), "practically dismantled his motel room, then tied four bed sheets together, strapped a fire extinguisher on his back, and leapt Tarzan-style off a fourth-floor balcony. . . . Instead of swinging to another balcony, however, his arc sent him crashing through a plate glass window and into a first-floor room. UCLA wound up with a $3,500 bill." The young man escaped serious injury.

The incident was bad enough in itself. But there was more to come. The athlete transferred to another school for a time and then returned to UCLA, but was dismissed after the 1977 track season. He finally enrolled at California State College-Long Beach, only to become angry with the coach there and threaten him with a beating, a threat that eventually earned him a month in jail.

Later, the Dallas Cowboys, because he had also been an All American defensive tackle while in high school, gave the young man a tryout. The club soon dropped him, however, on learning that he was awaiting trial for his trouble at Cal State.

Barry Lorge finished the athlete's story with the report: "Friends say that he is now a professional wrestler in Canada, awaiting a tryout with a Canadian Football League team."

Tragic as it was, the story at least did not end in death. The same cannot be said of two other stories. They're about the great European cyclists, Englishman Tommy Simpson and Frenchman Yves Mottin.

During a 1967 international race in France, Simpson

suddenly began to weave back and forth across the road in the middle of one lap. He fought to regain control, but then lost consciousness and pitched over on his side. He died several hours later without ever coming out of his coma. When an autopsy was performed, a heavy amount of the extremely potent amphetamine drug, methamphetamine, was found in his system. A vial of the drug was also discovered in his pocket.

The next year Mottin won a major French cross-country race. He collapsed and died two days later. Heavy amphetamine consumption was blamed for his death.

CONTROLS AND A HEALTHY
CHANGE OF DIRECTION

The growing heavy use of various drugs by athletes over the years has caused the sports world to adopt increasingly strict control measures. These measures have had an effect on the use of amphetamines. The amphetamines are now—and have been for a number of years— among the drugs that, if detected in the body during postevent urine tests, can cause an athlete to be disqualified from such competitions as the Olympics. In addition, the amphetamines have been carefully monitored and administered by the professional sports leagues in the United States since the passage of the Comprehensive Drug Abuse Prevention and Control Act in 1970.

Along with the United States, a number of other countries have adopted strict drug-control laws that have an effect on the use of amphetamines. One such nation is France. The French laws enabled the country to put two of cyclist Mottin's friends on trial for providing him with the amphetamines that took his life.

Fortunately, there seems to be a healthy change of direction in the amphetamine picture. Studies and the remarks of many athletes indicate that the drug's use in sports seems to have passed its peak. Though still alarmingly widespread, use reached its high point in the early 1980s and is now dropping steadily as more and more athletes are abandoning the amphetamines.

The factors mentioned above—from the postevent testing and the professional league monitoring to the strong government regulations—are given much of the credit for the declining use. As much, if not more, credit is given to the athletes themselves. More and more of them are taking seriously the word of just how efficiently these energy-giving uppers can damage a career and a life.

In addition to those just mentioned, there is yet another factor. It may well be the one most responsible for causing so many athletes to toss out their pills. It is an ironic fact that has come to light in the past few years. The amphetamines, despite releasing all that energy and confidence, have been found to contribute nothing to a victory.

Tests held after recent Olympic meets showed that the losers all had amphetamines in their systems. And the winners? Hardly a one of them showed a trace of the drug.

Whatever the leading cause may be, the decline is being happily watched by the sports world.

CHAPTER SEVEN

BRAKING
AND BOOSTING

The anabolic steroids have found a place in sports because they build new body tissue. In this chapter, we're
going to look first at some drugs that achieve a quite
different effect. They are called brake drugs. Their name
comes from their ability to retard—"put the brakes on"—
a certain type of body development.

Then we'll turn to a procedure that provides increased stamina. Here it is not a drug that furnishes the
stamina. Instead, the athlete's own blood does the job.
The process is called blood boosting.

THE BRAKE DRUGS

It is not definitely known whether brake drugs are used
in athletics. Rather, their use is strongly suspected. The
suspicion centers on many of the female gymnasts who
compete for the Communist-bloc countries. The suspicion is there because the gymnasts are of the size and
build of ten- or eleven-year-old girls. Yet they are in their
mid to late teens.

In *Death in the Locker Room,* Bob Goldman mentions three of the young women. Superb performers who
represented the Soviet Union when the 1978 Gymnastics Championships were held in France, they are Elena
Mukhina, Natalia Shaposhnikiv, and Maria Filatova. At the
time, Elena was age eighteen. Yet she stood just five feet

(152 cm) tall and weighed ninety-two pounds (42 kg). Both Natalia and Maria were seventeen. Natalia reached but four feet, nine inches (145 cm) and weighed seventy-nine pounds (36 kg). Maria was four feet, five inches (135 cm). Her weight was sixty-five pounds (29 kg).

What is to be gained from the suspected administration of brake drugs by team physicians and trainers? Quite simply, the drugs keep the Communist-bloc athletes small in a sport where smallness provides a winning edge. They do so by delaying the arrival of puberty, the age at which the female becomes capable of bearing children. When puberty is delayed, so are the physical changes that accompany it—the development of the breasts and the widening of the hips among them. These are changes that bring an increase in weight and a shift in the body's center of gravity, both of which affect the gymnast's performance adversely.

The drugs add to that winning edge in yet another way. The gymnasts have trained for several years as little girls. Were puberty allowed to occur, each gymnast would be placed at a disadvantage by having to accustom herself to the physical changes that it induced. The brake drugs not only permit her to compete for a time longer with a small body but also with one that is completely familiar to her.

A variety of drugs can be used for braking. Medically, they serve a number of valuable purposes, among them the treatment of certain cancers. Of the drugs that are perhaps being used in sports, two have come under particular suspicion—*medroxyprogesterone acetate* and *cyproterone acetate.* The term *acetate* means that the two contain a salt of acetic acid.

MEDROXYPROGESTERONE ACETATE
Medroxyprogesterone acetate is a synthetic drug that is derived from progesterone. Progesterone itself is an estrogen, meaning that it is a female hormone. The acetate is usually taken orally.

To understand the workings of the acetate, it is necessary to see the role that progesterone plays in the two

Members of the Soviet women's gymnastic team at the 1972 Olympic Games in Munich. Multiple-gold medal winner Olga Korbut stands on the far right. Observers of Eastern European female gymnasts have noted their increased growth rate and weight gain once the individuals reduced or ceased participation in the sport.

basic functions in the female reproductive cycle—ovulation and menstruation. When the female ovulates—passes an egg (the ovum) from one or the other of the ovaries to the uterus—progesterone is produced in the ovaries. The hormone prepares the lining of the uterus to hold and nourish an embryo should the egg be fertilized with a male sperm.

If there is no fertilization, the production of progesterone dips and the egg is freed from the woman's body through menstruation. Should the egg be fertilized, the progesterone continues to be produced at a significant level. The ovaries manufacture it for about three months, after which it is produced in the placenta, the membrane organ in which the fetus grows. The high level of progesterone keeps the mother from ovulating and menstruating again until after the child's birth. Since both ovulation and menstruation have to do with an egg that has yet to be fertilized, both are unnecessary during pregnancy.

Just as it does in the pregnant woman, a high level of progesterone suppresses ovulation and menstruation in a woman not pregnant. When they are suppressed in a girl at puberty, there is, at the same time, a suppression of the hormones that bring about the physical changes that go with womanhood. Those changes—increased breast and hip size—are needed to help the female ready herself to bear a child. But, without ovulation, there can be no child. So the body sees no need to advance into womanhood. The girl remains—as do the gymnasts thought to be receiving medroxyprogesterone acetate—a child in build and size.

In fairness, it must be stressed again that it is still only suspected that the Communist-bloc countries use brake drugs—but it is a suspicion that makes a great deal of sense. As a number of sports physicians have pointed out, the presence on the same teams of so many teenage athletes with the petite bodies of little girls gives rise to thought. Can it all be mere coincidence? It hardly seems likely.

On the other hand, it is quite possible that the rigorous diet and hours of hard training demanded in the Communist-bloc countries could account, perhaps totally or in very great part, for the petiteness.

A strict diet is certainly used by the Romanian women's gymnastics team, whose splendid Nadia Comaneci was a major star at the 1976 Olympics. In 1977, Comaneci and her teammates toured the United States. During the journey of two weeks, they ate just five meals. The meals consisted mainly of tomatoes and lettuce supplemented by vitamin pills.

The aim of the team's strict diet and rigorous training schedule is to keep a gymnast's fat content at less than 3 percent of her weight. This, the Romanian coaches feel, will postpone puberty and the unwelcome body changes that accompany it.

The Communist-bloc countries deny that their women gymnasts are given brake drugs.

CYPROTERONE ACETATE

Cyproterone acetate is a synthetic drug that is available in Europe but not worldwide. It is classed as an antihormonal substance. This means that it is able to curb the actions of various hormones.

One of the hormones against which it acts with particular success is testosterone, the male hormone at the base of many of the steroids. Since testosterone provides the male's sex drive, cyproterone acetate is widely prescribed in Europe to control the behavior of hypersexed (overly sexed) males. It is often ordered by the courts for men who have committed sex crimes such as rape, child molestation, and indecent exposure.

Sports doctors believe that cyproterone can be used as a brake drug for women because it is not just an antitestosterone agent but a general antihormonal drug as well. In women, it would block the action of the hormones responsible for their sexual growth.

BIRTH CONTROL PILLS

Though they are not actually brake drugs, birth control pills must be mentioned here because of their effect on the woman competitor's reproductive cycle. Many women athletes use them, but not for birth control purposes. Rather, the pills are taken to adjust the reproductive cycle so that women will not menstruate during times of competition.

BLOOD BOOSTING

Blood boosting, as was earlier mentioned, is a procedure that can be used for providing increased stamina. Also known in sports as blood packing and blood doping, it is based on the fact that our red blood cells carry the oxygen that provides us with energy and endurance.

The procedure stems from the work of a Swedish scientist, Dr. Bjorn Ekblom of the Stockholm Institute of Gymnastics and Sports. In a 1972 experiment on increased energy, Dr. Ekblom removed approximately a quart of blood from each of four subjects. He then separated the red cells from the blood and placed them under refrigeration. The subjects were given four weeks in which to replenish the lost blood. At the end of that time, Dr. Ekblom reintroduced the red cells into each subject. They joined the red cells in the replenished blood supply.

The result: The four subjects, each with an excess of red cells, had the energy to run longer on a treadmill before becoming exhausted. They displayed an increase of 25 percent in endurance.

A simple theory lay behind the Ekblom experiment. The muscles require oxygen to perform. The oxygen is carried in the red cells. The more red blood cells there are, the more oxygen there will be. Hence, longer performances can be had by adding to—boosting—the number of red cells. Technically, this approach is called *induced erythrocythemia*—the introduction of surplus red blood cells.

Dr. Ekblom carried out his experiment in the name of pure research. He did not intend that his procedure be actually used in competition. But because of the winning edge it promises, blood boosting has been tried in several sports throughout the years since 1972. It is said to work best in events that demand stamina for extended periods of time and that call for the prolonged repetition of the same muscle movements. Among the athletes who have experimented with the procedure are Nordic skiers in Europe, racing cyclists in both Europe and the United States, and weight trainers going after a record number of repeated actions at an increased speed. Boosting is not considered useful in events requiring short bursts of energy.

HEALTH QUESTIONS

At present, the benefits and ethics of blood boosting are being debated in the athletic world. Many sports doctors find the procedure a health hazard. For one, they argue that the danger of infection looms from the needles and other sources when the cells are being reintroduced into the system, especially when the infusion is not being carried out under medical supervision. Another of their greatest fears is that the muscles, performing beyond the time when exhaustion would be normally felt, will force the heart to pump too hard and suffer damage.

Other doctors feel that the procedure is reasonably safe when administered under medical supervision. For substantiation, they point to research that has been done at York University in Toronto, Canada. As reported in a 1985 issue of *Sports Illustrated,* the results of the research have tended to remove the fear that the heart will pump too hard to keep up with the constantly working muscles. The research found that, along with the other muscles, the myocardium (the muscle of the heart) receives an extra supply of oxygen. That extra supply helps the heart to cope with the excess strain.

There is one point, though, on which all sports physicians agree. They say that a *second* type of blood boosting is far more dangerous and should be avoided. In this procedure the athletes receive not their own blood but that of a friend or relative. Such transfusions pose the threat of needle infection (especially, again, if there is no medical supervision), plus the possibility that a perfectly healthy athlete will be infected with an illness carried by the blood donor—perhaps hepatitis, mononucleosis, or even AIDS (acquired immune deficiency syndrome).

ETHICAL QUESTIONS
From an ethical standpoint, blood boosting is widely regarded as unfair because of the strong edge it can give a competitor. But there are at present no laws specifically banning its use, neither on the world nor on the national scene. At the world level, the general drug policy of the International Olympics Committee (IOC) forbids the use of any "physiological substance" that is taken in "abnormal quantities" or by "abnormal" means for the sole intention of bettering athletic performance "in an artificial or unfair manner." In the minds of many sports authorities, blood boosting fits this category and so should be banned in the Olympics. However, the IOC has yet to institute such a ban.

The committee perhaps cannot be blamed for its inaction. A ban promises to be unenforceable—at least for the present. This is because there is, as yet, no reliable test for detecting the presence of "boosted" cells in an athlete's system.

At the national level, the United States Olympic Committee (USOC) has recently taken a strong anti-boosting stand. The stand came after a USOC investigation revealed in early 1985 that seven riders with the United States cycling team had used blood boosting during the Los Angeles Olympics. They did not receive reinfusions of their own blood but were given transfusions from donors. The transfusions were administered under medical supervision. Six of the seven transfusion recipients went on to win medals—one gold, four silvers, and one bronze. All together, in the best Olympic performance recorded by American cyclists since 1912, the team collected nine medals. The disclosure of boosting cast the shadow of cheating over the achievement.

News reports on the boosting revealed that it had caused much controversy within the team and within its sponsoring agency, the United States Cycling Federation. There were twenty-four riders on the team. Seeing the transfusions as dangerous or unethical, all but seven had refused them. Many of the antiboosting riders did not blame the seven for casting the shadow of cheating over the Olympic achievement, but rather pointed an accusing finger at the team coaching staff, which was headed by Edward Borysewicz, an assistant with the 1976 Polish Olympics team. The staff, the riders claimed, had pressured hard for the transfusions.

As for the Cycling Federation, two of its officers—president Rob Lea and secretary Deke Smith—resigned in anger on learning of the boosting. They looked on it as cheating. Other Federation and team officials, though several said that they did not like the idea, supported the boosting. They felt it was necessary if the American cyclists were to keep abreast of their Russian opponents. (Once more, the international political rivalries that have for so long stained the Olympics can be seen.)

The USOC's investigation into the boosting incident brought a sharp comment from Dr. Irving Dardik, chairman of the group's committee on sports medicine. Long an ardent foe of boosting, he said that the procedure, in the eyes of the USOC, is not only unethical and unacceptable but also illegal. Additionally, the USOC's medical director, Dr. Kenneth Clarke, has written a letter to the International Olympic Committee asking it to take a hard stand against boosting.

Such activity may soon see blood boosting, even without a reliable test for its detection, banned in both national and international competition. If so, Dr. Dardik will be more than pleased. Following the USOC investigation, the press reported him as saying:

"Anybody who tells me that removing athletes' blood or giving someone else's blood for transfusion into an athlete to try to improve performance is an okay thing to do—he's just nuts."

CHAPTER EIGHT

COCAINE:
THE DRUG OF
THE 1980s

It's time now to turn from the misuse of the medical drugs to the abuse of the so-called recreational drugs. In this chapter and the next, we'll be talking about cocaine and the damage it is doing in sports today. Then we'll give a chapter to the second of today's most abused recreational drugs, marijuana.

The lion's share of our attention is going to concentrate on cocaine rather than marijuana. There are three reasons for this.

First, the current abuse of cocaine, by both athletes and the general public, is known to be especially widespread. In fact, the abuse is so widespread that cocaine has come to be called "the drug of the 1980s."

Second, cocaine is being employed in sports in a way that marijuana is not. Though still classified as a recreational drug, it is no longer being sought by athletes just for the passing pleasure or escape from life's trials that it can provide. Many competitors are treating cocaine as if it were a medical drug. They are gambling that the energy it induces will give them that winning edge.

Finally, more than marijuana, it has written a particularly sad page in the sports history of the 1980s. It has either damaged or ruined several dozen fine careers in that time. They have been the careers of not only some of the world's best but also *best-known* athletes.

TOWARD THE 1980s

The Inca Indians of ancient Peru, as you'll recall from Chapter One, stirred the leaves of their coca plant in hot ashes and then held the mixture in their mouths when it cooled. The mixture deadened their tongues and—a miracle so far as the Indians were concerned—filled their bodies with great energy and erased the need to sleep. The Incas used the magical concoction for needed extra energy in sporting contests and especially when heading out on long hunts or into battle.

Responsible for the energy, of course, was cocaine. Classified today as a stimulant drug and known worldwide simply as coke, it is now understood to be so potent and dangerous that its production and traffic (except for a few medical purposes) are outlawed in a number of countries, the United States among them. It is a violation of United States federal law to cultivate, process, sell, or even possess cocaine. Conviction on any of these counts can bring stiff sentences—for instance, from several months to several years for possession, and from one to fifteen years for selling. The state laws against cocaine vary across the country. But they, too, can range from a few months in prison on a minor count of possession to years for a serious selling offense.

Long known only in South America, cocaine made its way, as we'll see later, to Europe and the United States in the late nineteenth century. It was not widely used in these areas for many years. In fact, it was such a stranger in the United States that it was rarely mentioned when today's drug abuse problem first took shape in the late 1950s and early 1960s. At that time, the nation's drug treatment centers saw but a handful of cocaine victims. The era's principal drugs of abuse were LSD, marijuana, and the amphetamines.

A coca plant

This situation changed, however, in the early 1970s. For reasons still not clearly understood today, cocaine caught on with segments of the American population and began to win an increasing popularity. Its popularity grew steadily until cocaine, instilling its feelings of great energy and a self-confidence to match, has become the principal drug of abuse in the 1980s. Today, the federal government estimates that between fifteen million and twenty million Americans have tried cocaine in recent years. Among them have been some of the nation's top sports stars.

Virtually all of those stars are to be found in the professional ranks. Why? Because cocaine is a highly expensive drug. In the United States, it usually sells for $100 to $150 a gram (.035 oz)—a price tag that puts it out of the financial reach of all but the richest of young and amateur athletes. Its costs are similarly high in Canada and Europe.

But just who in the professional ranks have had their careers and reputations damaged by cocaine?

COCAINE IN BASEBALL

Sports Illustrated, in a 1984 issue, answered that question as it applies to one sport: the country's national pastime, baseball. The magazine listed the names of sixteen major league players who had been convicted or treated for the abuse of hard drugs—cocaine, marijuana, alcohol, or some combination of the three—in the preceding five-year period. Included among the cases were the following:

1982 □ Outfielder Alan Wiggins of the San Diego Padres is arrested for the possession of cocaine. The charges against him are dropped when he completes the program at a CareUnit hospital in southern California. CareUnit Hospitals are a group of drug and alcohol rehabilitation centers. Baseball Commissioner Bowie Kuhn suspends Wiggins from play for thirty days.

1982–1983 □ During the 1982 season, Los Angeles Dodgers' relief pitching ace Steve Howe is treated at the Meadows, an Arizona rehabilitation center, for cocaine and alcohol abuse. Howe begins the 1983 season with fine appearances on the mound, but then checks into CareUnit for further treatment. While there, he is out of action for thirty days. Commissioner Kuhn, impatient with Howe's continuing abuse, fines him $53,867—an amount equal to the pitcher's salary for that thirty-day period.

1983–1984 □ First baseman Willie Aikens of the Kansas City Royals and his teammates, outfielders Jerry Martin and Willie Wilson, are convicted of attempting to buy cocaine. Sentenced at the same time is former Royals pitcher Vida Blue. They all serve eighty-one–day sentences at the Fort Worth Correctional Facility. Blue goes on to CareUnit for rehabilitation treatment. The four are suspended from play for a time by Commissioner Kuhn.

1984 □ Atlanta Braves pitcher Pascual Perez is convicted in his homeland, the Dominican Republic, on charges of possessing cocaine. He is suspended from professional ball in the United States for several months.

In 1985, a new scandal joined the ones above. At the end of a fourteen-day trial, a Pittsburgh jury convicted Curtis Strong, a caterer and former clubhouse cook, on charges of selling cocaine to major league players between 1980 and 1983. Specifically, Strong was convicted of selling the drug on eleven dates to four players. At the time of the trial, three of the players were with the Los Angeles Dodgers, the Cincinnati Reds, and the Kansas City Royals. The fourth was a former outfielder with the Pittsburgh Pirates. They all had been with different teams when the sales were made. During the trial, Strong was called "a traveling salesman of cocaine" by the prosecution. After the jury's verdict, Strong's attorney said that he planned to appeal the case later in the year.

THE FOOTBALL PROBLEM

The problem, of course, isn't limited to baseball. It has also reached into the ranks of professional football. In 1983, the Miami Dolphins' great running back, Eugene "Mercury" Morris, was sentenced to twenty years on charges of cocaine dealing. That same year saw four other players in the headlines for possessing cocaine.

They were defensive back Greg Stemrick of the New Orleans Saints; linebacker E. J. Junior of the Saint Louis Cardinals; and fullback Pete Johnson and defenseman Ross Browner, both of the Cincinnati Bengals. All were brought to court on felony charges of possessing cocaine. Stemrick and Junior were found guilty and given a year's sentence. Johnson and Browner won immunity from conviction by telling the court that they had made more than a dozen cocaine purchases from a dealer. Browner said that he had made from twelve to fifteen buys. Johnson admitted to approximately fifteen purchases.

National Football League Commissioner Pete Rozelle suspended the quartet for four games in the 1983 season. The suspensions meant a loss in pay of $25,850 for Stemrick, $33,350 for Junior, $34,600 for Johnson, and $37,600 for Browner.

In August 1983, Tony Peters of the Washington Redskins was one of seven people charged with conspiring to distribute cocaine. The defensive back entered a plea of guilty and was sentenced to two concurrent four-year prison terms. The sentences were suspended, however, and Peters was fined $10,000, placed on probation, and ordered to perform five hundred hours of community service. At the same time, he was suspended from NFL play. The suspension was lifted in the summer of 1984 because of his excellent conduct and community service while on probation.

BASKETBALL AND SOCCER

The recreational abuse of cocaine is reported to be present in the National Basketball Association. With cocaine being an illegal drug, no one can say how widespread the abuse might be, because it is carried on in secret. However, in 1979, the *Washington Post* interviewed several NBA players and found that they did not regard the abuse as a major problem. They said that the abusers kept their habits away from the basketball court, did not allow cocaine to interfere with the quality of their play, and were always clear-minded and ready to work at the opening buzzer. One player remarked that not many NBA cagers were "into coke."

These, of course, were the opinions of just a few players who might have been protecting the reputations of their league and fellow players. But one fact indicates that they might well have been painting an accurate picture. As of the time this book is being written, pro basketball has yet to be hit with a major cocaine scandal.

The mention of all the above cases is not intended to give the impression that the cocaine problem is limited just to the United States. Such is not the case at all. In recent years, a number of professional soccer leagues in Europe, alarmed at the rumors of the increasing player abuse of cocaine and other drugs, have begun to require saliva and urine tests of their teams. The tests are conducted without warning.

TWO POINTS TO REMEMBER

Two points should always be remembered about the above cases. First, while they are all tragic, it must be stressed that some seem to be ending on a positive, upbeat note. For instance, the conduct of defensive back Tony Peters while on probation certainly gave strong indication that he was putting his problem behind him. Outfielder Willie Aiken, when he returned to play with a new team—the Toronto Blue Jays—told reporters that his time in jail did him good by keeping him away from drugs and alcohol. Vida Blue, despite his team's poor record early in the season, pitched well for the San Francisco Giants in 1985.

Second, the cases must not lead to the impression that *every* professional baseball and football player abuses cocaine (or any other drug for that matter). Nor must there be the impression that *most* do. Both are mistaken and unfair ideas. Easily more than twelve thousand professionals have played both games during the cocaine era. They have come from varied backgrounds and brought with them diverse viewpoints on health and morality, and it is impossible to think that they have all decided in favor of drug abuse—or that even the majority of them have done so. There are just too many different kinds of personalities involved for that sort of thing to happen.

But then how widespread, really, is the cocaine problem? As pointed out before, no one can say because cocaine is an illegal drug and is abused in secret. Actually, the number of professionals arrested or treated for drug abuse of any kind makes the problem look rather small on a per capita basis—in one five-year period, for instance, only sixteen baseball players out of the several thousand who worked in the major leagues during that time.

The numbers look equally small in football. In 1975, Charles R. Jackson, the assistant director of security for the National Football League, pointed out some figures during a speech to a conference on drug control held at Saint Louis, Missouri. Jackson said that of the eight thousand players who had been under contract to the NFL, only thirty had been arrested for drug violations in the preceding five-year period. The arrests added up to less than .38 percent of the league's players.

Jackson went on to say that between 1970 and 1975, a total of eighty-six players—or 1.05 percent of the league's athletes—had been linked to drug involvement. Of that number, 70 percent had not been found guilty of the drug charges. The thirty arrests during the five-year period had involved twenty-nine players, with one player being arrested twice. All together, Jackson argued, the NFL's drug problem at the time was being caused by a very small percentage of players.

The number of arrests, however, cannot be used as a true measure of the problem. It is more than probable—indeed, it's most likely a certainty—that they do no more than indicate "the tip of the iceberg." As holds true of any type of lawbreaking, far more cocaine users have assuredly gone undetected than have been arrested. If so, then the cocaine problem can, indeed, be widespread in the pro ranks. Further, so far as the Jackson speech is concerned, it was made, remember, in 1975. The greatest increase in cocaine abuse has come since then. But whatever the true extent of the problem may be, it unmistakably looms large in the eyes of the two professional baseball leagues and the National Football League. All three have taken action against it and the entire problem of drugs in sports. We'll report their actions in Chapter Eleven.

Now let's take a close look at the drug that is causing the trouble and see just what it does to the athlete user.

CHAPTER NINE
COCAINE AND THE ATHLETE

Cocaine is one of eighteen alkaloids found in the leaves of the coca plant. It is, in fact, the major alkaloid present, accounting for about 0.5 to 1.0 percent of each leaf's weight. The drug seems to be nature's way of protecting the leaves from foraging animals. It is quite bitter to the taste.

(Alkaloids are substances present in certain fungi and plants. They consist of various elements, a principal one being nitrogen. They are poisonous, but can serve as powerful medicines when used carefully in small amounts.)

As for the coca plant itself, it can take the shape of either a tree or a bush. In appearance, it resembles somewhat the blackthorn bush of Europe and North America. But despite this resemblance, it grows almost exclusively in South America, both in the lowlands and along the slopes of the Andes Mountains. In general, it rises to a height of about eight feet (2.5 m), bears long and straight branches, and produces leaves that are colored a bright green on their tops and a pale gray-green on the undersides.

FROM BUSH TO POWDER

Cocaine is extracted from the leaves after they have been pulled from the plant. They are burned in a mixture of kerosene, sulfuric acid, and an alkali. The drug emerges as a sticky paste. The paste contains between 70 and 85 percent pure cocaine, with the remainder of the mass being made up of other coca alkaloids, plus some oil from the leaves.

Further processing—done with hydrochloric acid—transforms the paste into white flakes and lumps, both of which can be easily crushed to a fine powder. The powder is known as cocaine hydrochloride. The processing eliminates many of the alkaloids and much of the leaf oil. Left in the powder is a cocaine content ranging from 90 percent to a completely pure 100 percent. The degree of purity determines the potency of the drug and depends much on how well and carefully the processing has been carried out. Of course, the purer the cocaine is, the more potent it is.

As you know, cocaine is an illegal drug in many of the world's nations, the United States among them. But the drug itself is not widely used *everywhere* in the world. It finds its greatest popularity in Europe, Australia, and the Americas—Canada, the United States, Mexico, Central America, the Caribbean islands, and its homeland, South America. It is not widely used in the Middle East, Asia Minor, and Asia itself. In these areas, the chief drug of abuse is opium (which comes from the poppy flower of the opium plant and is the base substance for heroin), followed closely by certain types of marijuana, chief among them hashish.

The principal coca-growing countries are Peru and Bolivia. Because of today's massive demand for cocaine, coca cultivation is now under way in Brazil and Colombia.

Once the cocaine gum is obtained by the Peruvian and Bolivian growers, it is sent out of the country for processing into the white powder. Peru and Bolivia are agricultural nations that do not yet have the industrial means to do large-scale processing.

The main processing country is Colombia, a nation that has enriched itself over the years by processing and distributing illegal drugs of all types—from cocaine to marijuana and such chemical substances as the amphetamines. After being processed, cocaine is smuggled to the outside world in various ways—concealed on the persons of air and sea passengers, hidden away among the legitimate freight on airliners and cargo ships, and, especially for those shipments heading to the United States, packed aboard small boats and private airplanes.

The United States stands as one of the world's largest cocaine customers. The U.S. government estimates that from forty-eight to upward of fifty tons of the drug are smuggled into the country annually. For the most part, cocaine reaches the shores of the United States along the country's southern coast—from Florida on the east to Texas on the west. There are also several major destination points on the Pacific and Atlantic coasts, chief among them Los Angeles and San Francisco in the west, and New York City in the east. Once it has arrived, the drug is shipped throughout the country, again by various means—trucks, trains, commercial and private airplanes.

EARLY COCAINE USES

The South Americans early identified cocaine as a valuable medical drug. Its ability to deaden Inca tongues led to its use as an anesthetic in a number of ancient surgical operations.

On the other hand, when it was first introduced into Europe and the United States in the late nineteenth century, many physicians thought that its energizing effects could be put to use in the treatment of depression. Among them was the famous pioneer in psychoanalysis, Austria's Sigmund Freud. He took the drug himself and administered it to patients in need of having their spirits lifted.

Freud also noted that cocaine, in common with the amphetamines, has the power to curb the appetite. He prescribed it for certain digestive disorders. For a number of years, cocaine was medically employed in weight control.

Today, replaced by other drugs and widely banned in the world as dangerous, cocaine serves little medical purpose. It is pretty well limited to use as a local anesthetic in certain surgeries.

WHAT HAPPENS TO THE BODY

When now reading of how cocaine acts on the body, you may well think that you've turned the pages back to the chapter on the amphetamines. The effects of both drugs are so much alike as to be identical.

For instance, isn't there a familiar ring to these physical effects? The heartbeat quickens. The body temperature rises. So does the blood pressure. And, as just mentioned, the appetite diminishes.

And what of the greatest of all the cocaine effects— its tremendous thrust of energy? No sooner does cocaine enter the bloodstream than it hits the user with that energy and a sense of well-being that can mount to euphoria. At the same time, there is a flood of self-confidence—the surging belief that one is better than everyone else and able to handle any work or social situation that may arise.

There is one difference, however, between the cocaine and amphetamine highs. The amphetamine highs, you'll recall, can last from several hours to two or three days. The cocaine-induced energy and self-confidence fade in twenty to thirty minutes and disappear entirely a short time later.

But back to the similarities. The descent from the cocaine high matches that of the amphetamine's return journey. There is great tiredness and often the need to sleep. Especially for the steady user, there can be a frightening sense of depression, one that is frequently accompanied by intense irritability, nervousness, and restlessness.

To overcome the descent problems, longtime users imitate amphetamine victims by taking alcohol, sedatives, Quaaludes, and even heroin to calm themselves. Then, in common with the amphetamine victim, they find themselves in a vicious circle of "uppers and downers."

Depressed to the point of being unable to become energetic on their own, they reach for cocaine for the trip to pleasure and confidence; then reach for the "downers" to ease the return to normal; and then reach again for cocaine for another ride up.

PROLONGED AND HEAVY USE

Pointing out yet another similarity to the amphetamines, recent research indicates that small amounts of cocaine taken at widely separated intervals do no more harm than the light use of alcohol or cigarettes. It is the prolonged and heavy use of the drug that invites trouble.

The trouble matches that caused by undisciplined amphetamine use: insomnia, a deepening depression, paranoid fears and behavior, and hallucinations. Physically, with the appetite perennially curbed, there can be a dangerous weight loss and a lowering of the body's resistance to disease. In time, the liver cells can be harmed. And as time passes, there can be the increasing danger of a heart attack. Finally, from the very first days of use, there is the ever-present threat of death from overdose.

And now a final comparison with the amphetamines: As is the case with them, medical science does not yet know for certain whether heavy cocaine use is physically addictive. But like the amphetamines, and for the same reason, cocaine is widely suspected of being psychologically addictive. Many steady and heavy users at last reach the point where they feel unable to function without its help.

Cocaine holds at least two special threats for the user, no matter whether he or she is new to or well ac-

Keith Hernandez of the New York Mets was named as a witness in the 1985 cocaine-distribution trial of former caterer Curtis Strong.

quainted with the drug. They are present because of the ways cocaine is taken: by hypodermic injection or inhalation. Hypodermic injection is made possible by the fact that cocaine is soluble in liquid. Inhalation, which is popularly known as "snorting," works in two ways. Either the user sniffs the powder up the nose or breathes in the fumes from a heated cocaine solution.

With cocaine being an illegal drug, injection is dangerous because it is usually self-administered. Dirty needles are often used (as is also true with other drugs of abuse). They threaten infection and the chance of passing on a disease carried by a previous user. As for inhalation, it sends the drug to the bloodstream via mucous membranes in the nose. On passing through, the cocaine constricts the blood vessels, reducing the blood supply and drying up the nose. Ulcers can form after a while on the membrane tissues. The nasal septum is then apt to break open and form little holes in one or more spots. The little holes can be closed only with surgery.

HOW COCAINE WORKS

Even today, doctors are uncertain over the question of how cocaine works to energize the body. A leading theory is that cocaine, like many other stimulant drugs, produces an action on certain body chemicals when it enters the bloodstream. These chemicals are called *neurotransmitters*. The cocaine prompts them to activate the nerve cells and send tiny electrical impulses coursing through the nervous system.

The impulses affect various body functions, such as the heartbeat, and pour in on at least two areas of the brain—the hypothalamus and the cerebral cortex. The hypothalamus controls such physical operations as the body's temperature and such emotions as anger and fear. The cerebral cortex governs a number of our mental activities.

As a result of this invasion of impulses—so the theory goes—the brain turns into something like an overloaded telephone switchboard when all the electrical impulses come pouring in. It simply cannot respond to all the "incoming calls." As a consequence, the body and the brain become overly energized.

As we did with the anabolic steroids and the amphetamines, we come at last to that all-important question: Why have a number of famous and highly paid sports stars, with everything to lose, risked the dangers of cocaine? The answer is to be found in the two roles that cocaine plays in sports—first, as an abused recreational drug and then as a misused winning-edge drug.

COCAINE'S RECREATIONAL ABUSE

In the world at large, today's cocaine abuse is seen mainly among adults. The reason is that cocaine, to recall a point made in Chapter Eight, is a highly expensive drug. Though its price tag varies from time to time, with much of the charge depending on the amount of the drug being made available to the illegal market, cocaine usually sells for between $100 and $150 per gram (.035 oz) in the United States. A cocaine habit can cost an American user dearly—say, from $500 to between $2,000 and $5,000 a week. Prices are just as stiff in Canada and Europe.

Its price tag puts cocaine beyond the financial reach of all but the wealthiest young people. Likewise, its cost is too much for countless adults earning an average wage. Yet, many of them take cocaine on a steady basis and sacrifice any number of life's necessities to satisfy their habit. The drug, however, is most often found among high-income professional people.

Drug authorities think that cocaine is highly popular among the nation's affluent professional people for reasons other than the mere fact that they can afford it. A belief here is that the drug provides relief from the tensions created by high-salaried work and the complex personal and social responsibilities that almost invariably accompany it. Another belief holds that a number of high earners are users because, despite their respected positions and large incomes, they actually have little confidence in themselves or their abilities. They like and need the sense of superiority and the feeling of "being up to anything" that cocaine induces. And, returning to the idea of cost, some authorities say that many users first try cocaine so that they can gain the status that comes of being able to afford so expensive a drug.

The above points can all be easily transferred to the sports world. Cocaine is beyond the financial reach of most amateurs and so is found principally in the professional ranks. As is true of the world at large, it is abused recreationally for reasons quite aside from the fact that the professional players can handle its cost.

Dr. Joseph Pursch of CareUnit Hospitals, a group of rehabilitation centers, pointed to one very basic reason in a 1983 issue of *U.S. News & World Report* magazine. He said that many professional players not only have a great deal of money but also plenty of free time on their hands. They spend much of each season uprooted from home and living in hotel rooms. They are often handed drugs by fans and admirers. The slide into a ruinous drug habit for recreational purposes—for just passing the empty and restless hours when not at work—can come all too easily.

There are other reasons just as basic. To see and feel them, you need only put yourself in the professional's place. There's all that money. There's all that fame. There's all that public adulation. And there are all those constant demands made on you by the team, by the fans, and by yourself. Win. Outperform your opponent so that your salary is earned and your pride maintained. Never let down. Especially never let down because if you do, there's always someone waiting to step in and take over your job.

Again, the slide into a harmful recreational cocaine habit can come all too easily for any number of reasons—all the way from trying to live in the "fast lane" because of your money and fame to forgetting the pressures of your life and feeling, for a few too-quickly passing moments, that you're as heroic as you're supposed to be.

COCAINE FOR
THAT WINNING EDGE

But there is something new in the cocaine picture. There was a time when its use in sports was solely for recreational purposes. Now, however, things are changing. More and more, cocaine is being tried as a medical drug. Players are turning to it in the hope that its energy will give them that cherished winning edge.

In particular, this change has been seen in professional football. As several sports doctors have pointed out, cocaine's pain-killing capability is especially liked in this game of bruising, crunching body contact. As the player users see it, the drug, like the amphetamines, enables them to withstand more pain than they could endure without it. They say they can hit harder and absorb harder hits.

For many players, the drug is replacing the amphetamines. The reasons given for the switch are various. The players say that cocaine does not confuse the thinking as much as the amphetamines do. They find the trip back down to normal—at least in the beginning stages of use—easier than it is from an amphetamine high. And, again in the beginning phases of use, cocaine's aftereffects do not strike them as being as severe as those of the amphetamines.

Some players like the drug because its effects are of shorter duration than those of the amphetamines—twenty to thirty minutes as opposed to several hours or even two or three days. They get their "high" only for the length of time that it is really needed and not for long hours after the final gun. One player commented that users look on cocaine as a "second half drug," to be taken when tiredness and the aches of all the continuing hard body contact are at their worst.

News reports suggest that the misuse of cocaine as if it were a medical drug looms at its worst in football and baseball, the one because of the vicious contact, the other perhaps because of the exceedingly long and arduous season, with both bringing a cumulative sense of tiredness and pain. But there are signs that the misuse is spreading to track. One sign: A woman coach recently called the Olympic training facility in Colorado to ask a question. What, she wanted to know, could she do about someone who was urging her runners to try a sedative for a good night's sleep before a meet and then take some cocaine in the morning for the extra pep to be needed that day.

Cocaine as a winning-edge drug does not seem to have made much headway in professional basketball. As was pointed out in Chapter Six, Paul Silas has observed that the pro game is too fast and demands too much quick thinking for anyone to risk being on the amphetamines. Since cocaine is likewise a stimulant drug, we can reasonably assume that the players feel the same way about it. In the main, cocaine in the National Basketball Association has been reported as being abused as a recreational drug. But, as you'll recall from Chapter Eight, the players who were interviewed by the *Washington Post* in 1979 felt that the abuse was kept well away from the courts and was not especially widespread.

CHAPTER TEN

MARIJUANA

Cocaine may be so widely used today that it is called "the drug of the 1980s." But the fact is that marijuana is even more widely abused. Studies have led the United States government to estimate that upward of twenty-five million American adults and young people—approximately 12 percent of the nation's population—have used marijuana regularly, meaning at least once a month. That total far outstrips the fifteen to twenty million Americans reported to have tried cocaine in recent years.

Marijuana's great popularity stems much from its low cost. The drug comes in varying grades of potency. At the time this book is being written, the charge per ounce (28 g) can run to about $200. Some lower grades can be had for between $36 and $60 an ounce, while still lower grades can be obtained even more cheaply. Contrasted with cocaine's price tag per gram (.035 oz) of $100 to $150, marijuana costs next to nothing.

Because it is so inexpensive, marijuana is especially popular among young people. A 1982 survey of some 17,700 high school students in the United States revealed it to be their favorite drug. In Canada, a 1981 study came up with the fact that about four million young people over age eighteen had tried marijuana and that two million had turned to it at least once in the preceding twelve-month period. The study also reported that more than half of all Canadian high school students had sampled the drug.

Like cocaine, marijuana is outlawed in many parts of the world. In Europe, it is illegal in all countries but one—Spain. Its cultivation, sale, and possession are banned throughout the United States. Federal penalties for trafficking in more than one thousand pounds (454 kg) of the drug can bring a fine of $125,000 and up to fifteen years in prison for a first offense. The fine can jump to $250,000 and the prison sentence to twenty years for a second offense. State marijuana laws vary greatly, with possession of a small amount—perhaps an ounce or two—usually being considered a misdemeanor that can result in a fine of several hundred dollars and/or a jail sentence of a few weeks or months. Major trafficking offenses are apt to earn prison sentences of one year to life.

Despite the nation's antimarijuana laws, about ten thousand to fifteen thousand tons of the drug are smuggled to American users each year. The tonnage has an estimated value of more than $24 billion. Mostly, the drug is brought in from other countries. An increasing amount, however, is being grown within the United States itself.

DAMAGED CAREERS
AND REPUTATIONS

Countless Americans have been arrested, imprisoned, or otherwise punished over the years for using and/or selling marijuana. Among those most damaged by their marijuana involvement have been athletes whose reputations easily match those caught in the nation's cocaine scandals.

To name but a few: In 1973, NFL Commissioner Pete Rozelle charged the Los Angeles Rams' brilliant wide receiver, Lance Rentzel, with personal misconduct, including the illegal possession of marijuana, and suspended him from play for the season. The 1980s opened with shock for baseball fans when they heard that catcher Darrell Porter of the Kansas City Royals had gone to a rehabilitation center for treatment of alcoholism and a drug dependency. Revealed was the story of a gifted player who felt so pressured to succeed throughout his life that he had sought escape not only in drink but in marijuana, amphetamines, and eventually cocaine. Shock erupted again in 1984 when running back Chuck Muncie was handed a season's suspension from the NFL after failing a urine test during negotiations that would have sent him from the San Diego Chargers to the Miami Dolphins. The chief chemical in marijuana was detected in his urine. Muncie had twice been treated for drug dependency in 1982.

One of the saddest of all stories belongs to Orlando Cepeda, for seventeen years a superb National League first baseman and hitter. In a career that saw him make up the heart of the San Francisco Giants' batting order (with Willie Mays and Willy McCovey) and take the St. Louis Cardinals to the 1967 World Series, Cepeda amassed a splendid record—more than 2,100 games, 2,351 hits, 379 home runs, and 1,365 RBI (runs batted in). In 1961, he led the league in both home runs (46) and RBI (142). For leading the Cardinals to the World Series with a .325 batting average, 25 home runs, and 111 RBI, Cepeda was named 1967's Most Valuable Player in the National League.

When he retired, he did so as a national hero, both in the United States and his homeland, Puerto Rico. But then came a day in 1978 at Puerto Rico's San Juan airport. Cepeda and a friend walked into the freight terminal and collected a box sent to them from Colombia. Police and drug agents closed in on the pair and took possession of the crate. On being opened, it was found to contain 165 pounds (75 kg) of marijuana worth about $66,000.

Arrested and charged with importing and possessing marijuana, Cepeda was sentenced to five years in prison. He served only nine months of the term, but has been paying heavily in lost reputation ever since. Along with the late Roberto Clemente, he was once the pride of Puerto Rico. Further, he came from the island's most respected baseball family; his father had been known as the Babe Ruth of Puerto Rico. Today, Cepeda is the target of scorn and anger there. It is as if the people feel that his drug involvement betrayed the whole country after he had brought them such honor.

Cepeda recently told a reporter that he thinks his people will never forget what he did.

At the time of this book's writing, Cepeda is living on his baseball pension and supplementing his income with speeches. His home is a modest one in Los Angeles. He hopes one day to establish a string of baseball camps for young people. He tried to start one such camp in Puerto Rico, but was unable to win government approval for the project.

WHAT IS MARIJUANA?

Marijuana is one of the names given to the chemicals in a yellowish resin found in the hemp plant. Known in botany as the *Cannabis sativa L,* the plant thrives in temperate and tropical climates and thus can be found in wide-ranging areas of the world. It grows in Asia—in China, Japan, and Korea, and westward from India to Lebanon. It is to be found in such European countries as France, Hungary, Italy, and Yugoslavia. In the Western Hemisphere, the growing areas are located in Central and South America, Mexico, and the United States. The plant seems able to thrive almost anywhere in the United States. The heaviest domestic cultivation is reported to take place in Hawaii, California, Oregon, North Carolina, and West Virginia.

The plant usually grows to a height of ten to twenty feet (3 to 6 m). It sprouts long, flowering branches which, in their turn, sprout leaves that run from three to ten inches (8 to 25 cm) long. Both the male and female hemp plants contain some sixty-one chemicals, with one—tetrahydrocannabinol (THC)—being the chief source of marijuana. The male plant, however, contains but a small THC content. The female plant is responsible for the major share of the world's marijuana supply.

Cannabis plant

The drug is obtained from the upper parts of the plant—from its stems, flowers, flower seeds, and leaves. Marijuana, as just mentioned, comes in various strengths. Those strengths are determined by the amount of THC produced in individual plants or plant strains. The most potent marijuanas are bhang, ghanga, and hashish. They are cultivated mainly in Asia.

For marketing, the plant's resinous parts are crushed into a greenish tobaccolike substance. The drug is then usually smoked, in a pipe or as a cigarette. It may also be mixed in food or liquid. One of marijuana's many nicknames, tea, springs from the early Asian practice of mixing the drug in various brews, chief among them tea. Numbered among its other nicknames are pot, grass, weed, and Mary Jane.

The hemp plant has been helping the world since ancient times. From it has come a tough fiber that has gone into the manufacture of rope, clothing, ship's caulking, sacking, and paper, Historians believe the plant originated in Asia, in an area north of the Himalayas. They know that the Chinese were cultivating the plant for its fibers as early as 2800 B.C. They theorize it made its way west to Europe in about A.D. 500. It traveled farther westward with the early American colonists.

The *Cannabis sativa L* continues to be of economic service today. Its fiber is used in the production of rope. Its seeds go into the manufacture of paints and varnishes.

As for marijuana itself, it, too, has been known since ancient times. It was early put to work in medicine, in great part because of its ability to induce a state of dreamy relaxation in the user. Shen Nung, the Chinese emperor whose studies four thousand years ago opened the way to the modern development of the amphetamines, also investigated the cannabis plant and said that its resin could be of value in the relief of such varied problems as emotional upset, constipation, gout, beriberi, and even absentmindedness. A number of ancient cultures, among them India, used the drug's relaxing effects to treat nervousness and depression.

Western medicine learned about marijuana in the early nineteenth century. For the remainder of the century, it was sought for the treatment of various physical and psychological complaints, depression being a chief representative of the latter. In our century, marijuana has been replaced by other medical drugs and is rarely employed for the ill, especially in the Western world. At present, however, one marijuana drug—delta 9 tetrahydrocannabinol—is under medical study. A laboratory-produced drug derived from marijuana's chief chemical, it is being researched for possible work in controlling the nausea and vomiting triggered by the chemotherapy treatments given cancer patients. The synthesized drug is also being considered as an agent for reducing the within-the-eye pressure that marks the presence of glaucoma, a disorder that, if not controlled, leads to blindness.

THE MARIJUANA HIGH

Marijuana hits the user in much the same way as alcohol. It interferes with the smooth functioning of the brain and brings on a state of intoxication. But it is an intoxication that differs from the drunkenness of alcohol in a very basic manner.

Drunkenness can affect a person in various ways—from a silly happiness to an equally silly sadness to an intense and even dangerous anger. Marijuana intoxication—the drug's high—usually follows a set pattern and ends in a specific way. To begin, there is a feeling of restlessness. Next, there is a growing sense of well-being. The user then enters the dreamy state of relaxation that was mentioned earlier.

A number of physical reactions occur as the pattern develops. The blood pressure goes up. The heartbeat quickens. The pupils of the eyes dilate. The flow of saliva drops, often bringing on a sudden thirst. The thirst is usually for water rather than alcohol, juices, or soft drinks. Just as often, there is a sudden hunger.

Marijuana is classified as a hallucinogen (a drug that

causes the user to hallucinate) because of some specific effects that may be encountered as the high progresses. For one, the vision may distort and cause surrounding objects to assume strange shapes and sparkling colors. Likewise, one's hearing may begin to misbehave. Commonly, the user "hears" bells ring and "buzzers" go off. The human voice often sounds unreal, as though echoing out of a barrel or coming from a great distance. The sense of time is also often affected, with everything going into slow motion and making seconds seem like long minutes.

Small amounts of marijuana trigger these visual and auditory tricks. Full hallucinations—the "seeing" of things that aren't there—arrive with heavier amounts. As is true of the amphetamines and cocaine dosages, a very heavy intake of marijuana can induce toxic psychosis, with the victim hallucinating wildly and imagining that "bugs" are everywhere to be seen.

The hallucinations sound frightening. But not the drug's other effects, mainly that dreamy state of relaxation. They, in fact, sound pleasant. But there is evidence to show that they are sometimes anything but pleasant. Users have reported sudden feelings of restlessness, fear, and physical upset during highs. One user, for example, recalled that his head seemed to have turned into a balloon and was ready to burst at any moment.

To date, drug studies have not settled the question of whether marijuana is physically addictive. But the drug is widely thought to be psychologically addictive. The belief here is that, in time, habitual users cannot relax and put aside life's burdens for a time without marijuana.

There is also the belief that long-term abuse alters an individual's view of life in an unhappy way. Said to be damaged through being blunted are such qualities as self-esteem, personal ambition, and desire to succeed. The change in personality resulting from long use of marijuana interferes with the user's overall ability to function successfully in the everyday world.

As for long-term physical damage, physicians point out that marijuana is usually smoked. It poses the same dangers to the lungs and heart as does tobacco. ⌐

MARIJUANA IN SPORTS

Unlike cocaine, marijuana plays just one role in sports. It is abused in the search for pleasure and relaxation or as a means of escaping from reality for a time. It is not used as a winning-edge drug.

The reason is obvious. The state of dreaminess produced by its high renders marijuana useless as a winning-edge drug. The user moves slowly and clumsily. Reaction time slows and the hands lose their steadiness. Good perception goes out the window, what with all those visual tricks being played by the drug. In short, the user has neither the mental sharpness nor the physical agility to be anything but helpless in the hands of an alert opponent.

In two ways, however, a number of athletes use marijuana as if it were, at least in part, a winning-edge drug.

First, as you know, some turn to it on the trip down from an amphetamine or cocaine high, easing the journey downward so that they can recover all the more quickly for their next competition date. And some use marijuana to relax prior to competition, usually taking the drug during the preceding evening for a good night's sleep. Doctors say that the sleep is apt to do no good. The user often awakens feeling unwell, as though suffering an alcoholic hangover.

On reaching this point in the book, we've come to the end of our look at the drugs found in sports. We're ready for the last of the five questions that were asked many pages ago in Chapter One:

What is a worried sports world doing to curb or end its problem of drug misuse and abuse?

CHAPTER ELEVEN
WORKING TO STOP THE PROBLEM

The sports world is working along five fronts to curb and perhaps one day end the drug problem in its midst. Those five fronts are: drug testing, monitoring, education, rehabilitation, and disciplinary action. All five fronts are blended together in various drug prevention programs, but they can be discussed individually.

DRUG TESTING

Major amateur competitions in such sports as weight lifting, cycling, and track-and-field have been seeking out the presence of drugs in athletes for more than twenty years. They have done so, as you know, through the use of saliva and urine tests, with most of the emphasis being placed on the latter. When the tests detect the presence of a forbidden drug in an athlete's system, it can result in the competitor being banned from the competition or deprived of his or her victory medals.

The most stringent of all drug-testing programs is carried out at the Olympic Games. Olympic officials began testing for drugs in 1967. At the time, they were principally interested in such winning-edge drugs as the amphetamines, but added the anabolic steroids to their list of forbidden substances in 1973. Today, more than three hundred drugs are banned by the Games.

To see just how stringent the Olympic testing program is, we need only look at the procedures used in the 1984 Games at Los Angeles. The Los Angeles Olympic Organizing Committee assigned a representative to each event. Immediately after any event, the representative summoned the first-, second-, and third-place winners, along with another competitor picked at random. They were escorted to a nearby drug-testing station, or, as it was called, a doping control station. There, each athlete gave two samples of urine.

One sample was stored away under strict security in case it would be needed later. The second sample went to a laboratory maintained by the International Olympic Committee, there to be tested. If the test proved negative—that is, if no forbidden drug revealed itself—all was well. But if the result came up positive, a medical committee immediately informed the athlete and his or her team officials of the finding.

A second analysis was then carried out in the presence of International Olympic Committee representatives and officials from the athlete's team. If it, too, proved positive, the athlete was stripped of his or her medals.

Similarly tough testing measures are employed by such major competitions as the Pan American Games and the various European championships. Testing in the United States is done in many national, state, and regional amateur events.

TESTING IN PROFESSIONAL SPORTS

Urine testing is presently a subject of heated controversy in professional sports. It is favored by some in the pro ranks and opposed by others. Commissioner Pete Rozelle of the National Football League opposes the idea, as do many football, baseball, and basketball players. At the core of the opposition are several beliefs—that testing will be too costly and time-consuming, that it will be impossible to enforce because of player opposition, and that it is unnecessary because the antidrug programs long sponsored by the various leagues are prov-

ing successful without it. We'll be discussing those programs in just a moment. Most players see the testing as
an invasion of privacy and say that, as professionals, they
should not be burdened with it so long as they are doing
their jobs well.

As a general rule, testing is not used in the major
sports leagues. But there are exceptions. In baseball, for
instance, there is no mandatory testing, but in 1984, the
Players' Association (the players' union) and the Major
League Baseball Player Relations Committee (representing management) reached an agreement that contains provisions for testing in certain circumstances. The
agreement, which deals with all aspects of how players
with drug problems are to be treated medically and/or
disciplined, permits a recommendation for testing when
a player is under drug treatment or is charged with a
drug problem by his team. The recommendation cannot
come from the team, but only from a special committee
assigned to study all such cases. Called the Joint Re-
view Council, the committee is made up of three members who are "neutral" in the case and who should have
special professional knowledge and experience in drugs.

Early in 1985, the newly appointed commissioner of
baseball, Peter Ueberroth, announced a plan for testing
all personnel in the major and minor leagues, except
major league players. The major league players were not
included because they and their Association have long
objected to the idea of testing on the grounds that it is
an invasion of privacy. However, in the wake of the mid-
1985 drug scandal involving Curtis Strong (see Chapter
8), a growing number of major leaguers said they no
longer objected to the test and that its use might be
necessary to help end the drug problem in baseball.

THE LEAGUE DRUG PROGRAMS
—THE FIRST DAYS

By the dawn of the 1970s, today's drug problem was
widespread among the public and was fast gaining
ground in the sports world. At the time, the drugs caus-

*Baseball commissioner
Peter Ueberroth*

ing the greatest alarm in athletics were the amphetamines, soon to be joined by the anabolic steroids. As you'll recall from Chapter Five, the amphetamines, even though they had required a doctor's prescription since soon after World War II, were being freely dispensed in professional locker rooms because their dangers were not yet fully appreciated and because their use was not yet sternly curtailed by the government. Then came the government's Comprehensive Drug Abuse Prevention and Control Act in 1970 and with it the requirement that the prescribing of the amphetamines be very strictly regulated.

An example of what was first done in professional sports in response to the alarm and the Act comes from baseball. In December 1970, the Association of Professional Baseball Physicians met to discuss the use of drugs in athletics and issued a statement condemning the use of any stimulant that was taken to improve performance. In less than a month, the then commissioner of baseball, Bowie Kuhn, called for a study of drug usage in the pro game. A later report from the commissioner's office (1973) said that the study found baseball to be "largely free of drug problems" (a statement that conflicts with Johnny Bench's autobiography *Catch You Later,* with its recollections of widespread amphetamine use at the time). The report, however, went on to say that, because of the overall public drug abuse—especially by young people—it was felt that a continuing antidrug program should be launched to protect the game in the future.

The commissioner's office was particularly concerned about the drug problems of many of the young players who would be entering the professional ranks in the coming years. The report said that "approximately 500 young men come into professional baseball for the first time each year."

Accordingly, the beginning of an antidrug campaign—called Baseball's Drug Education and Prevention Program—began to take shape. The report said that "baseball was the first professional sports organization to adopt such a program" and then went on to explain that three seminars were held during spring training in 1971. Attending were administrative personnel from all the major league clubs, managers, coaches, and player representatives. They were briefed on the program and on the dangers that drugs posed for professional sports. From there, word of the program went out to all major and minor league personnel.

Baseball may have been the first sport to adopt an antidrug program in response to the new government regulations, but professional football was just as active in 1971. The National Football League adopted what came to be called its Drug Control Program. The National Basketball Association launched a program of its own, while the National Hockey League established a strict antidrug policy. The leagues have resembled each other in their efforts. They have all sought to combat the drug problem through the use of four methods. Some leagues have employed all four methods. Others have used some combination of the four. The methods are: monitoring, education, rehabilitation, and disciplinary action.

DRUG MONITORING

The term drug monitoring applies to the winning-edge medical drugs that can be legally used with a doctor's prescription. It means that the sports organizations keep close track of how such drugs are dispensed and in what amounts. But just how do the groups get the job done? The National Basketball Association and the National Football League provide two representative examples.

To oversee its antidrug program, the National Basketball Association employs a physician who is an expert in drug matters. The teams provide him with complete inventories of their prescription drug supplies. He checks the inventories before and throughout the season. The inventories enable him to judge whether team physicians are authorizing the drugs in normal or excessive amounts. Whenever a player receives a prescription drug, a notation is made of it in his medical file. The notation specifies the date of the prescription, the dosage, the doctor's name, and the reason for the prescription.

In the National Football League, the office of Commissioner Pete Rozelle requires each team to keep a detailed record of all the prescription drugs on hand throughout the season. Each team must submit this record to the commissioner's office at both the beginning and end of the season, with the first due by July 15 and the second by the following January 16. Also, each team must present a monthly record of the prescription drugs purchased throughout the entire year. The operating head of each team is responsible for submitting the records. As in the NBA, the doctor in charge of the league's drug program is able to judge whether any team is prescribing the drugs to excess.

Further, the players are required to inform their teams of any prescription drugs obtained from outside sources, regardless of whether the medications are given for a minor complaint or in the wake of serious surgery.

When the records or reports from other directions— say, from players troubled by the misuse around them— indicate a team's excessive use, the commissioner may take any of a number of steps. These range from investigating the matter and warning the team to calling for strong disciplinary action. One of the toughest disciplinary actions to date was leveled against the San Diego Chargers in 1974.

That year Mr. Rozelle's office heard complaints from several players that amphetamines had been overprescribed for the Chargers during the 1973 season. An investigation proved to his satisfaction that one of the team doctors had prescribed the drugs in excess for eight players between August 2 and November 6, 1973. The investigation ended with disciplinary actions in the form of fines.

The Charger team was fined $20,000 for failing to supervise its administrative personnel. General Manager Harland Svare received a fine of $5,000 for failing to exercise proper supervisory controls over his players and staff. The eight players involved in the scandal were handed fines ranging from $1,000 to $3,000. In total, the fines came to $40,000. The doctor who had overprescribed the amphetamines was discharged.

DRUG EDUCATION

Drug education in the league programs is aimed at two targets—the team personnel (not only players but also trainers and all other personnel) and the general public.

To reach the two targets, the leagues have engaged in a wide variety of activities over the years. A firm idea of how various those activities are can be had by looking at a representative few. Here are some examples of the work that has been done with team personnel in baseball and football:

1971 □ Soon after Commissioner Bowie Kuhn holds the three seminars to inform managers and staffs of baseball's new antidrug program, a booklet goes out to everyone in organized ball. Titled *Baseball Vs. Drugs,* it has been checked for accuracy by the Federal Bureau of Narcotics and Dangerous Drugs. The booklet describes the baseball antidrug program.

1972 □ Commissioner Kuhn's office prepares a thirty-minute color film on drugs and their dangers. It is distributed to all teams for viewing by their personnel. The teams also make the film available for showings to high schools, colleges, and community groups.

1972 □ Drug authorities are invited to speak at sixteen National Football League teams during the training and regular seasons. Nine clubs have their team physicians speak to the players. Other teams bring in physicians from nearby universities, plus representatives of state and local law enforcement and drug agencies.

1972 □ The NFL sends representatives from each of its clubs to a drug abuse educational course at Washington, D.C. Conducted by the White House Special Action

Office for Drug Abuse Prevention, the course lasts three days. The representatives take the information gathered there back to their teams.

1981 □ Recognizing the difficulties in identifying the players with drug problems because the players often keep them a secret and deny their presence, the NFL employs former Minnesota Viking star, Carl Eller, to serve as a part-time consultant to the league. His job: to meet with team coaches and administrators and point out the signs of drug misuse or abuse. He also works with a number of players. Eller is himself a man who once suffered and then overcame a drug problem.

1982 □ Concerned by reports of the growing sports misuse of the anabolic steroids, Commissioner Rozelle sends a letter to all NFL players, reminding them of the league's attitude toward the steroids. He writes: "The League recognizes that in certain circumstances physicians may prescribe anabolic steroids for valid medical reasons. However, if these drugs or similar compounds are taken by otherwise healthy players . . . with the intent merely to achieve increased body bulk, strength, stamina, or similar physical and athletic attributes, such actions will be deemed a misuse and will be dealt with under the provision in each player's contract which prohibits 'stimulants or other drugs . . . to enhance on-field performance.'" Mr. Rozelle then comments on the steroid risks uncovered by research.

1983 □ NFL coaches attend a workshop on drug dependency held at the Betty Ford Center at the Eisenhower Medical Center in Rancho Mirage, California. The workshop's aim is to help the coaches sight drug problems in players and other team personnel.

Similar work has been done in the National Basketball Association. At annual meetings, team physicians, general managers, coaches, trainers, and players are informed of the latest findings in drug research, with steps then being urged to acquaint all Association personnel with the dangers of drugs. The doctor in charge of the NBA drug program periodically conducts seminars for all personnel. He is also available to everyone for advice and consultation. Booklets and pamphlets on drug abuse are made available throughout the NBA.

When the drug education programs are directed to the public, they are aimed in great part at the nation's young people. Again, the activities are widely varied. And, again turning to pro football and baseball, here are some examples of what has been done:

1971 □ The NFL begins a cooperative effort with three government agencies to produce a series of antidrug spot announcements for airing during telecasts of league games. Fifty-eight players appear in the spots. An estimated one billion fans view the presentations. Twenty-six players appear in the following year, reaching a cumulative audience estimated at two billion. They urge volunteers to step forward and help to combat drug abuse and other social ills. The three government agencies are the National Clearinghouse for Drug Abuse Information, the National Center for Voluntary Action, and the Justice Department's Bureau of Narcotics and Drugs.

1971 □ At the request of President Richard Nixon, all major league baseball clubs participate in October's National Drug Abuse Prevention Week. Sixty-two players present radio and television spot announcements during the World Series and also make personal appearances at various functions connected with the Week. An estimated audience of 140 million see or hear the announcements. For their work, Commissioner Kuhn and the sixty-two players receive certificates of appreciation from President Nixon.

1972 □ The Dallas Cowboys distribute over thirty thousand antidrug posters to the twenty-six junior high schools in their area. They do so through a series of school assemblies that feature a film or an appearance by a

Cowboy player, a former addict, a drug enforcement officer, or a physician. The Cowboys produce an additional one hundred thousand posters for national distribution.

1975 □ A twenty-page booklet entitled *Drugs in the Game of Life* is prepared for distribution at Super Bowl IX. It is inserted into the one hundred thousand copies of the game's program. Contained in it is information on the Comprehensive Drug Abuse Prevention and Control Act, penalties for possession of drugs, and facts about the various abused drugs. The NFL prints additional copies of the booklet and makes them available to high schools, colleges, and community groups.

1984 □ Representatives from baseball, football, basketball, and other sports groups join the National High School Athletic Coaches Association and the federal Drug Enforcement Agency in a drug abuse prevention program. The program is aimed at over five million student athletes in some twenty thousand high schools.

As indicated by the above program, professional sports leagues are not the only organizations involved in anti-drug campaigns, Much activity also takes place at the amateur level. In addition to the work done by the National High School Athletic Coaches Association, community organizations and schools across the nation sponsor drug prevention projects, with the schools also providing much classroom instruction in the subject. For many years the National Collegiate Athletic Association has made a booklet on drug abuse available to coaches and athletes.

REHABILITATION

Both the amateur and professional leagues have taken a sympathetic view of players with drug problems. Long prevailing has been the view that the players are troubled with a diseaselike problem. The idea has been to help them through counseling and medical treatment rather than punishment.

To this end, the professional leagues sponsor recovery programs. They bring in physicians, drug experts, and former users, such as Carl Eller, to work directly with troubled players. They send the most troubled players to rehabilitation centers for treatment. The treatment—at least, on the player's first trip to a center—and the care that must often follow it are usually paid for by the leagues. One of the best of these programs is seen in the National Football League.

For a number of years, the NFL teams usually sent drug cases to nationally known centers such as the CareUnit Hospitals or the Hazeldon Foundation, which is located at Center City, Minnesota. But in 1982, Commissioner Rozelle urged a change. Saying that the centers were often too far away from a team's home city to be comfortable for either the team or the player, he urged each club to locate a center in its home area. He further asked that each club retain a local physician who is an expert in drug matters and who would be quickly available for advice and assistance. Since then, his suggestion has been put into effect throughout the league.

The Rozelle plan was refined in a December 1982 labor agreement between the NFL Players' Association and the NFL Management Council. The agreement called for the league to employ the highly respected Hazeldon Foundation to evaluate the local centers used by the teams so that "the highest degree of care and treatment" would be assured. The agreement also required that a player's problem and treatment be kept strictly confidential. Today, the Hazeldon Foundation, which is noted for its drug research as well as its drug education and treatment programs, continues with the work set forth in the agreement. Also, foundation counselors travel to training camps to explain and warn about cocaine and other drugs.

In addition to sponsoring rehabilitation efforts, the leagues depend on the doctors in charge of their programs for help. The physicians at the head of the NBA,

NFL, and baseball programs are readily available for consultations with the teams and individual players. The NBA maintains a telephone hotline for use by any player seeking advice or faced with a drug crisis.

As reported in a 1983 issue of *Newsweek* magazine, at least one major professional club has been helping matters along with a program of its own. The report described the work of a support and self-help group that Coach Sam Rutigliano of the NFL's Cleveland Browns had organized two years earlier. *Newsweek* said that the group, called the Inner Circle, consisted of eight drug-troubled players who met every Monday for counseling and discussions of how they were working to solve their problems. Present at the meetings to lend assistance were Rutigliano, a psychiatrist, a religious adviser, former Browns stars, and two highly respected nonuser players—Paul Warfield and Calvin Hill. During the two preceding summers, the Inner Circle members received drug education and counseling at rehabilitation centers. The program was proving a solid success.

Newsweek reported Rutigliano as being justifiably proud of the Inner Circle. He described it as being made up of players who are winning the fight of their lives.

DISCIPLINARY ACTIONS

Though the professional sports leagues continue to be sympathetic toward drug users, there has been a toughening of their outlook in the mid-1980s. The toughness is directed not at first-time cases but at users who cannot rid themselves of their problem after treatment or long-term counseling. The tendency is growing to discipline continued misuse and abuse through fines and suspensions from play.

Hitherto, such fines and suspensions were limited to players whose abuse got them into trouble with the law, as was the case in the 1983 suspensions of the Washington Redskins' Tony Peters, the St. Louis Cardinals' E. J. Junior, the New Orleans Saints' Greg Stemrick, and the Cincinnati Bengals' Ross Browner and Pete Johnson (see Chapter Eight). Five years earlier, defensemen

Don Reese and Randy Crowder of the Miami Dolphins had been suspended from the NFL on being found guilty of trafficking in drugs. After serving one-year prison terms, they were ruled eligible to reenter the league on the provision that each contributed $5,000 of his first year's salary to a Florida drug rehabilitation center.

The mid-1980s, however, have been marked by such cases as those of pitcher Steve Howe and running back Chuck Muncie. Former baseball Commissioner Bowie Kuhn, as you'll recall from Chapter Eight, fined Howe the equivalent of thirty days' pay—$53,867—when the pitcher went to a rehabilitation center for the second time in two months. In 1984, Muncie was ordered to undergo drug evaluation and comply with any prescribed treatment— or be suspended from play.

The toughening attitude stems from two sources. The first is the spread of cocaine misuse and abuse in the professional ranks in recent years. The various leagues fear that it will severely damage the reputations of their games and that countless shocked fans will soon be unwilling to come out and watch, as one football official has put it, "a bunch of millionaire coke heads trying to do their thing." Equally great is the fear that player users might try to pay off their debts to their dealers by throwing games or giving the dealers a gambling edge by informing them of team injuries.

Second, there is a feeling that rehabilitation centers, while helpful, are not the complete answer to a player's drug problem. Most center treatments last about four weeks and are usually followed by an indeterminate period of post-treatment care and counseling at the player's home base. Four weeks or so of actual treatment cannot be expected to cure a long-standing and deeply embedded habit—unless the patient tries very much to help himself. The leagues seem to feel that they cannot go on returning him to the centers indefinitely. Sooner or later, the player must take the responsibility to help himself.

The only other answer, then, seems to be to discipline continuing users and hope that it helps awaken them to what they must do for themselves. As Pete Rozelle said in *Newsweek* recently, he tells players that the NFL will pick up the bill for the first stay at a rehabilitation center. Then he warns them not to "mess up" again.

The new toughness is presently causing much controversy in the professional sports world. It is an attitude supported by many nonuser players. They have grown tired of the behavior and problems of users who seem unable or unwilling to help themselves and who are, in one player's words, "giving the rest of us and the game a bad name." On the other hand, a 1983 issue of *Sports Illustrated* severely criticized the fining of Steve Howe and said that such punishments would drive the athletic misuse and abuse of cocaine underground and discourage many players from stepping forth, admitting their problem, and asking for help.

It must be noted, however, that the National Hockey League has long held a strict policy toward drug abuse and that the league has had but two known cases of abuse over the past few years. The NHL's policy was firmly stated in 1978 by league president John Ziegler, when he announced, "Any player presently in the NHL or who may hereafter join the NHL must face the fact that if he wishes to be involved in illegal drugs then he will, if discovered, lose his privilege of playing in the NHL."

The statement was made immediately after President Ziegler had suspended Don Murdoch of the New York Rangers from play for one season because of drug possession. According to the NHL, there has been only one other instance of drug abuse by a player since then. In 1983, defenseman Ric Nattress of the Montreal Canadiens was given a season's suspension for the possession of illegal drugs.

President Ziegler eventually reduced Murdoch's suspension to forty games, and the Nattress suspension to thirty games.

A FINAL NOTE

Can testing, monitoring, education and rehabilitation programs, and disciplinary actions curb—or perhaps even end—the misuse and abuse of drugs in both amateur and professional sports?

At the moment, there is no way of telling. Often the measures seem to be succeeding. Often they seem to be failing. But whatever the successes and failures may be, the misuse and abuse continue to spread through the sports world at all levels. More than one player and coach—Cleveland's Sam Rutigliano among the latter—has likened the spread to a cancer. Only time can tell when and how the cure will come, as assuredly it must if sports are not to be irreversibly harmed.

In the eyes of many athletes and fans, the cure can come only if the above measures are joined by a new public attitude toward sports. They feel that athletics have become competitive in all the wrong ways during the latter half of this century. The accent has been too much on victory—so much so that it has become victory at any cost. At both the amateur and professional levels, the winners are overidolized and the losers overscorned. At the professional level, the athletes are made into highly paid warriors, with the pay rising higher and higher with their every win. At the amateur level, the international competitors are also made into warriors—soldiers who must prove the strength and nobility of their country by winning.

All these factors are exerting tremendous pressures on the athletes and driving many to the misuse of the winning-edge drugs and to the abuse of the recreational drugs. Added to the pressures are those that dedicated athletes impose on themselves—the pressures always to perform at their best and to prove themselves champions.

As so many athletes and fans now see it, these pressures must somehow be reversed. Perhaps, with all the money involved, it may be too late to reverse those at the professional level. But there is a strong feeling that much can be done at the amateur level and that everyone can lend a hand. Sensible people can demand that the politics be taken out of international competitions. Sensible parents and friends can teach the very young that sports are for fun, that winning isn't everything, that

a Little Leaguer needn't perform like an adult professional, and that good sportsmanship and graciousness
in defeat are characteristics that have been admired
everywhere throughout history. As they grow older, athletes can be urged to see that, while they'll always want
to do their best, there is no real victory when it is won at
the risk of a ruined health through drugs.

Perhaps if we all can learn and communicate these
lessons, sports will be able to go on being what they were
always intended to be—healthful, exciting, and happy
contests of skill and prowess.

What do you think? And what do you think you can
do to help?

FURTHER READING

The following books, booklets, magazine and newspaper articles, and special materials were used in the preparation of this book. Most of the published works are available at local libraries and should prove of interest and value to anyone who wishes to learn more about the problems that drugs pose both inside and outside the world of sports.

BOOKS AND BOOKLETS

American Medical Association, Department of Drugs (in cooperation with the American Society for Clinical Pharmacology and Therapeutics). *AMA Drug Evaluations,* 3d edition. Littleton, Massachusetts: PSG Publishing, 1977.

Drug Enforcement Administration, U.S. Department of Justice. *Drugs of Abuse,* July 1979. A publication containing articles from the magazine, *Drug Enforcement.* It features articles on the nature and action of narcotics, stimulants, depressants, and cannabis.

Goldman, Bob, with Patricia Bush and Ronald Klatz. *Death in the Locker Room.* South Bend, Indiana: Icarus Press, 1984.

Kruskemper, Hans L. *Anabolic Steroids.* New York: Academic Press, 1969.

Mirkin, Gabe. *The Sportsmedicine Book.* Boston: Little, Brown, 1978.

MAGAZINE AND
NEWSPAPER ARTICLES

Axthelm, P. "Cocaine Crisis in NFL." *Newsweek,* July 25, 1983.

Boswell, T. "Number of 'Poppers' in Baseball Grows Fewer Each Season." *Washington Post,* May 28, 1979.

Brady, D. "Rozelle Sets NFL War on Crime." *Washington Post,* June 6, 1980.

Brubaker, B. "A Pipeline Full of Drugs." *Sports Illustrated,* January 21, 1985.

Cooper, D. L. "Drugs and the Athlete." *International Drug Report,* April 1978.

DuPree, D. "Basketball Players Are More Attracted to 'Recreational Use.'" *Washington Post,* May 28, 1979.

International Drug Report. "Summary Report Baseball's Drug Education and Prevention Program." May, 1978.

Kaplan, J. "Taking Steps to Solve the Drug Problem." *Sports Illustrated,* May 28, 1984.

Lorge, B. "Chemical 'Edge': A Long History Behind Search." *Washington Post,* May 27, 1979.

———. "Particular Risks for Women Cited." *Washington Post,* May 27, 1979

———. "The Pressure Is On to 'Pop.'" *Washington Post,* May 28, 1979.

———. "NFL Drives Pills Underground; Users Find Them." *Washington Post,* May 29, 1979.

Lorge, B. and T. Boswell. "Steroid Effects Debated While Use Proliferates." *Washington Post,* May 27, 1979.

Maisel, I. "The Stuff I Did Was Enough to Kill You." *Sports Illustrated,* May 28, 1984.

McNicoll, A. "The Case Against the Decriminalization of Cannabis." *International Drug Report,* October 1978.

Morga, C. "Drugs and the Athlete." *International Drug Report,* May, 1978.

Power, G. "The Drug Scene in Sports: Who, What, How and Why." *New York Times,* October 19, 1975.

Rostaing, B., and R. Sullivan. "Triumphs Tainted with Blood." *Sports Illustrated,* January 21, 1985.

Runners World. "Drugs and Athletics." June 1983.

Sporting News. "Will Fines Curb the Use of Drugs in Pro Sports?" July 11, 1983.

Sports Illustrated. "Back to the Dark Ages." July 11, 1983. (Included in the feature column, Scorecard, edited by Jerry Kirschenbaum.)

————. "Is This the End of Chuck Muncie's Road?" September 24, 1984.

————. "A Lab Discovery Not Intended for Sports." January 21, 1985.

Stoler, P. "The Toughest Test for Athletes." *Time,* June 25, 1984.

Todd, T. "The Steroid Predicament." *Sports Illustrated,* August 1, 1983.

U.S. News & World Report. "Behind Drug Crackdown in Pro Sports." August 8, 1983.

SPECIAL MATERIALS

The following special materials were made available through the kind cooperation of the major sports organizations listed below.

Major League Baseball Player Relations Committee:
"Memorandum of Agreement" (the agreement reached between the major league baseball clubs and the Major League Baseball Players Association regarding procedures to be followed in cases of player drug dependency)

The National Football League:
"The NFL and Drug Abuse Prevention"
"NFL Drug Program"
"Important Events in NFL's Effort to Combat Drug Problems"
"Statement from Commissioner Rozelle"

National Hockey League:
Letter describing the NHL's antidrug policy

Office of the Commissioner of Professional Baseball:
"Summary of Baseball's Drug Education and Prevention Program"

INDEX

Aikens, Willie, 75, 77
Alkaloids, 80
Amateur sports
  anti-drug efforts, 100–101, 110
  politicization of, 40–42, 70
Amphetamines, 12, 46
  abuse of, 48–52, 58–59
  deaths from, 51, 59–60
  decline in usage, 60–61
  effects of, 30, 45, 48
  history of, 44–45
  laws concerning, 47, 57, 60, 104
  legal use of, 53
  medical uses, 45, 47
  popularity, reasons for, 54, 56
  in professional sports, 54, 56–58
  psychological hazards, 50–51,
    58–59
  weight loss with, 47, 53
Anabolic steroids, 12
  abuse of, 14–15, 26–32
  chemical makeup, 21
  coaches, dispensed by, 20
  disqualifications due to, 17, 19
  experimentation with, 16–17
  extent of use, 19–21, 32–33
  medical opinions about, 23–24,
    26
  medical uses, 15, 16
  "must win" personality and, 35–
    37, 43
  NFL letter concerning, 108
  political aspects of, 40–42
  pressures to win and, 37–38, 40–
    42

United States, usage in, 42–43
  warnings about, 32, 34
Androgenic drugs, 28–29
Anti-drug campaigns, 102, 104–5
Athletic mind-set, 37

Ball Four (Bouton), 49
Baseball, professional
  anti-drug campaign, 102, 104–5
  drug education program, 107,
    109
  drug testing in, 102
  drug usage in, 56, 74–75
Bench, Johnny, 56
Birth control pills, 66–67
Blood boosting, 12, 67–70
Blue, Vida, 75, 77
Borysewicz, Edward, 70
Bouton, Jim, 49
Brake drugs, 12, 62–63, 65–67
Browner, Ross, 76

Cannabis plants, 94, 95, 96
Catch You Later (Bench), 56
Cepeda, Orlando, 93–94
CIBA Pharmaceutical Company, 42–
  43
Clarke, Kenneth, 70
Cleveland Browns, 112
Coaches, 20, 110
Cocaine, 7, 12, 71
  abuse of, 83–84, 86
  athletes, attraction for, 88–90
  cost of, 74, 87
  effects of, 83, 86–87

Cocaine (*continued*)
  extent of usage, 78–79
  history of, 10, 73, 82
  laws concerning, 73
  medical uses, 82–83
  popularity of, 74
  processing of, 80–82
  in professional sports, 74–79, 87–89
  rehabilitation programs for, 77
  smuggling routes, 82
Cocoa plants, 72, 80
Comaneci, Nadia, 66
Compulsive personalities, 35–37, 43
Cortisone, 22
Crowder, Randy, 113
Cyclists, 59–60, 70
Cyproterone acetate, 66

Dallas Cowboys, 109–10
Dardik, Irving, 70
Death in the Locker Room (Goldman), 14, 27, 29, 36, 62
Decker, Mary, 8
Diet, 66
Disciplinary actions, 112–14
Diuretics, 27
Dope, 11

Education programs, 107–10
Ekblom, Bjorn, 67
Eller, Carl, 108
Ephedrine, 44
Estrogens, 29
Ether, 11

Filatova, Maria, 62–63
Freud, Sigmund, 82
Fugett, Jean, 57

Goldman, Bob, 14, 27, 29, 32, 36, 62
Gymnasts, 62–63, 64, 65–66

Hanley, Daniel, 32–33
Hernandez, Keith, 85
Hicks, Tom, 11
Hill, Calvin, 112
Hitler, Adolf, 41
Hoffman, Eric, 28
Hormones, 21
Howe, Steve, 75, 113

Inner Circle, 112

International Olympics Committee (IOC), 69

Jackson, Charles R., 78
Johnson, Pete, 76
Junior, E. J., 76

Korbut, Olga, 64
Kuhn, Bowie, 74, 75, 104, 107, 109, 113
Kuznetsov, Viktor, 17

Lea, Rob, 70
Lorge, Barry, 4, 53, 58

Mandell, Arnold, 56
Marijuana, 7, 12
  addiction to, 98
  athletes, use by, 92–94, 99
  effects of, 97–99
  history of, 96–97
  laws concerning, 92
  medical uses for, 97
  popularity of, 91–92
  processing of, 94, 96
Martin, Jerry, 75
Media coverage of sports, 38
Medical drugs, 6–7, 89–90. *See also* Amphetamines; Anabolic steroids; Brake drugs
Medroxyprogesterone acetate, 63, 65
Mirkin, Gabe, 36
Monitoring programs, 105–7
Morris, Eugene "Mercury," 76
Moses, Edwin, 9
Mottin, Yves, 59, 60
Mukhina, Elena, 62–63
Muncie, Chuck, 93, 113
Murdoch, Don, 114
"Must win" personality, 35–37, 43

National Basketball Association (NBA)
  anti-drug campaign, 105
  drug education program, 108–9
  drug monitoring program, 105–6
  drug usage in, 57, 76–77
  rehabilitation program, 111–12
National Drug Abuse Prevention Week, 109
National Football League (NFL)
  anti-drug campaign, 105

National Football League (*cont.*)
   drug education program, 107–8,
     109–10
   drug monitoring program, 106–
     7
   drug usage in, 54, 57, 76, 78–79
   rehabilitation program, 111, 112
National High School Athletic Coaches
   Association, 110
National Hockey League (NHL), anti-
   drug policy of, 105, 114
Nattress, Ric, 114
Nitroglycerine, 11
Nixon, Richard M., 109

Olympic Games
   blood boosting ban, 69–70
   drug testing for, 100–101
   politicization of, 41–42
Owens, Jesse, 41

Pacifico, Larry, 14–15, 26
Paranoia, 50–51
Perez, Pascual, 75
Peters, Tony, 76, 77
Porter, Darrell, 92–93
Pressures to win, 37–38, 40–42, 115–
   16
Progesterone, 63, 65
Pursch, Joseph, 88

Recreational drugs, 6–7. *See also*
   Cocaine; Marijuana
Reese, Don, 113
Rehabilitation programs, 77, 110–12
Rentzel, Lance, 92
Rozelle, Pete, 76, 92, 101, 108, 111,
   113
Rutigliano, Sam, 112, 115

San Diego Chargers, 106–7
Shaposhnikiv, Natalia, 62–63

Shen Nung, 44, 96
Silas, Paul, 57
Simpson, Tommy, 59–60
Slupianek, Ilone, 17
Smith, Deke, 70
Soccer, 77
Speed, 45
"Speedballs," 11
Stemrick, Greg, 76
Steroid bloat, 27
Steroids. *See* Anabolic steroids; Tes-
   tosterone steroids
Strong, Curtis, 75
Svare, Harland, 106

Testing for drugs, 100–102
Testosterone, 66
Testosterone steroids, 22, 28–29
Tetrahydrocannabinol (THC), 94
Thomas, Clayton, 19
Tkachenko, Nadezhda, 17
Tuokko, Markku, 17, 19

Ueberroth, Peter, 102, 103
Unborn children, hazards for, 29
United States Cycling Federation, 70
United States Olympic Committee
   (USOC), 69, 70

Warfield, Paul, 112
Weight lifters, 16, 25, 28, 39
Wiggins, Alan, 74
Wilson, Willie, 75
Winning, overemphasis on, 115–16
Winning-edge drugs, 7, 10–12
Women
   anabolic steroids and, 28–30
   brake drugs and, 62–63, 65–67
Wright, James, 20

Ziegler, Dr. John, 42–43
Ziegler, John (NHL president), 114